THE BEST IN TENT CAMPING:

WASHINGTON & OREGON

A Guide for Campers Who Hate RVs, Concrete Slabs,
and Loud Portable Stereos

THE BEST IN TENT CAMPING:

WASHINGTON & OREGON

A Guide for Campers Who Hate RVs, Concrete Slabs, and Loud Portable Stereos

Jeanne L. Pyle

Menasha Ridge Press

Printed in the United States of America
Published by Menasha Ridge Press
Second edition, first printing April 1996
Second edition, second printing May 1997

Library of Congress Cataloging-in-Publication Data

Pyle, Jeanne L., 1954–
The best in tent camping, Washington & Oregon : a guide for campers who hate RVs, concrete slabs, and loud portable stereos / Jeanne L. Pyle. — 2nd ed.
p. cm.
Includes bibliographical references (p. 164)
ISBN 0-89732-211-8
1. Camp sites, facilities, etc.—Washington (State)—Guidebooks. 2. Camp sites, facilities, etc.—Oregon—Guidebooks. 3. Camping—Washington (State)—Guidebooks. 4. Camping—Oregon—Guidebooks. 5. Washington (State)—Guidebooks. 6. Oregon—Guidebooks.
I. Title.
GV191.42.W2P95 1996
647.94747′09—dc20

96-6846
CIP

Cover design by Grant Tatum
Cover photos by Dennis Coello
Cover models: Christopher and Laurie Leman

Menasha Ridge Press
700 South 28th Street, Suite 206
Birmingham, Alabama 35233

CONTENTS

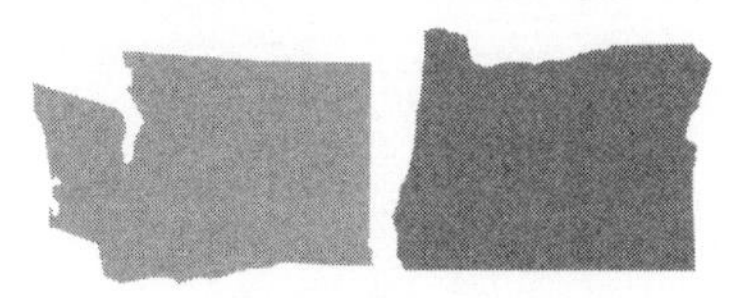

Appendices

PREFACE

It is always a bold and dangerous move to proclaim that something is "the best" without automatically assuming that there will be hell to pay for saying so. I suspect that will be the case with this book.

Having driven the miles, sampled the accommodations, amassed the notes and, finally, written the book, I have to admit that this modest collection of campgrounds is hardly the last word on quality car-camping options in Washington and Oregon. There are, after all, several thousand established campgrounds from which to choose in this vast, two-state area.

Undaunted by the statistics, however, and spurred on by a publisher with a deadline, I quickly formulated a plan of attack that was predicated on one critical element: my gut instinct. That, combined with my own knowledge of the Pacific Northwest environs, conversations with many people much more knowledgeable than I, access to oodles of reference materials, and a bit of dumb luck, steered me to the final list presented here.

The minimal criteria for selection—accessible by automobile and preferably not overrun by RVs, great scenery, and as close to a wilderness experience as possible—were quickly met by many of the campgrounds in the initial phase of my research. Plenty to choose from if I was looking for "The Encyclopedia of Car Camping," but far too many for the handy little pocket guide I envisioned.

Voila! The rating system! This method not only helped me narrow the field of contenders to a manageable herd, but it also gives you a quick reference to the characteristics you want in a campground (explained more fully in the following Introduction).

Even with the rating system, however, there were still many qualified campgrounds that suffered the heavy hand of subjectivity and had to be eliminated from this volume. Each of you probably has a list of favorites that could fill a book, too. Well, to me, "best" is just another way of saying favorite. So consider that I'm sharing my favorites and that this is simply the starting point for guiding you to new or rediscovered places. If you'd like to share some of your favorites with me, write to me at the publisher's address. Who knows? Even tent camping guidebooks can have sequels, can't they? The title's a cinch—*More of the Best in Tent Camping*. Stay tuned.

—*Jeanne Louise Pyle*

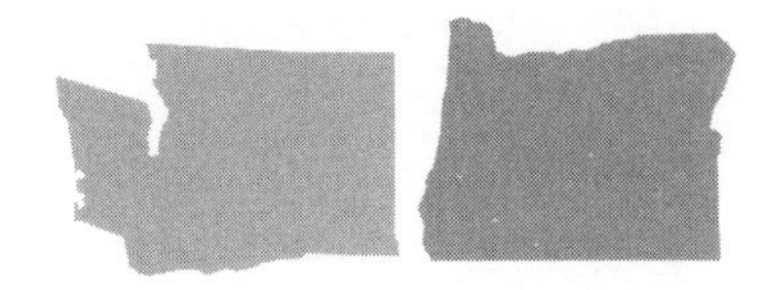

INTRODUCTION

A Word about this Book and Northwest Camping

From rocky coastlines to alpine meadows to sagebrush deserts, the Pacific Northwest is a region of unparalleled beauty and diversity. Extremes of climate, terrain, and vegetation can be experienced in just a single day's outing. The campgrounds included in this book are representative of the variety that makes the Northwest such a prized destination for those who seek outstanding outdoor adventures.

If you feel as I do that the quality of the adventure is greatly enhanced by the lack of RVs, this book is for you. If you feel as I do that the venerable car-camping tradition in this country has taken a back seat to the RV influence long enough, read on.

Granted, RVs are a fact of life in the Northwest just as they are everywhere else. It's the increasing trend to accommodate their presence that probably disturbs me as much as the convenience-crammed, gas-guzzling, road-hogging contraptions themselves.

I am willing to allow that the RV is probably a pretty useful mode of travel if you're going to spend a year on the road and want to avoid bankrupting on hotel rooms. But c'mon, folks! Do you *really* need all those creature comforts for a quick weekend in the hills or at the shore? I have to question your need to "get away from it all" when you take all of it with you into the wilds.

Speaking of wilderness, you may recall that this was one of the criteria for choosing the campgrounds in this book. Although Washington State is second only to Alaska in designated wilderness acreage, and Oregon is not far behind, more and more people are flocking to the scenic splendors beyond city limits and pushing the definition of a true wilderness experience.

Following a "20-mule team" caravan of RVs up a narrow, winding mountain road and falling asleep to the rumble of generators, one has to wonder if wilderness isn't more a state of mind these days than an actual place. For some campers, it is satisfaction enough just to pitch a tent alongside several hundred others in midsummer at the busy, nearby state park. For others, simply being able to drive to the campground immediately eliminates it from consideration. If your sentiment lies somewhere between these two extremes, you should find the offerings in this book appealing.

Here is some information that will prove useful whether you are a first-time camper in the Northwest or a veteran who can always use a few reminders.

West versus East

For a traveler, the most distinctive feature of the Northwest is the difference in climate, terrain, and to some degree, lifestyle between the western and eastern regions of both Washington and Oregon. For the purposes of this book (and because you will find it on most maps of the area), the Pacific Crest National Scenic Trail is the dividing line. It begins on the United States/Canada border and follows the spine of the Cascade Range down through Washington and Oregon to its end at the Mexican border.

Weather

Mark Twain once remarked, "The pleasantest winter I ever spent was a summer on Puget Sound." That pretty much sums up the prevailing conditions year-round (with a few exceptions) in western Washington and Oregon. Cool and damp is the general rule. Not so much rain, actually, as a healthy supply of gray clouds. Late summer and early fall are the most dependable for a lovely string of dry, sunny, warm days.

In eastern Washington and Oregon, conditions are desert-like, with hot and dry summers. Severe thunderstorms can be the biggest threat to outdoor activity in summer. At higher elevations on both western and eastern mountain slopes, snow is not uncommon even in midsummer.

Road conditions

Many of the campgrounds in this book are reached by minimally maintained access roads. Since we were looking for spots that are somewhat off the beaten path (and away from the routes those dreaded RVs travel), access roads can be rougher than you might expect. Check current road conditions before venturing too far if you are unsure of what you may encounter. And be sure that you have a good current road atlas with you. The maps in this book are designed to help orient you—nothing more. Although we've provided directions at the end of each entry, you'll still need detailed maps to get in and out of most of the campgrounds.

Restrictions

More people using an area usually means more restrictions. State and federal agencies manage most of the campgrounds in this book. Check with the proper authorities for current regulations on recreational activities such as permits for backcountry travel, licenses for hunting and fishing, mountain bikes in designated areas, etc. We have included some restrictions in the Key Information sections of each campground description, but because restrictions can change, you still need to check before you go.

Fires

Campfire regulations are subject to seasonal conditions. Usually there are signs posted at campgrounds or ranger district offices. Please be sure you are aware of the current situation and NEVER make a campfire anywhere other than in existing fire pits at developed sites.

Water

Many of the campgrounds in this book are remote enough that piped water is not available. No matter how remote you may think you are though, don't risk drinking straight from mountain streams, creeks, and lakes. Northwest waters are full of a nasty parasite called *Giardia lamblia*, which causes horrific stomach cramps and long-term diarrhea. If you don't have drinking water or purification tablets with you, boil any untreated water for at least five minutes. This will seem like a hassle if you're dry as a bone at the end of a long day of activity, but believe me, it's worth the few minutes of waiting for the agony you will avoid.

The rating system

Within the scope of the campground criteria for this book—accessible by car and preferably not by RV, scenic, and as close to a wilderness setting as possible—each campground offers its own characteristics. The best way to deal with these varying attributes was to devise a rating system that highlights each campground's best features. On our five-star ranking system, five is the highest rating and one is the lowest. So if you're looking for a campground that is beautiful and achingly quiet, look for five stars in both of those cate-

gories. If you're more interested in a campground that has excellent security and cavernous campsites, look for five stars in the Site Spaciousness and Security categories. Keep in mind that these ratings are based somewhat on the subjective views of the author and her sources.

Beauty

If this category needs explanation at all, it is simply to say that the true beauty of a campground is not always what you can see but what you can't see. Or hear. Like a freeway. Or roaring motorboats. Or the crack, pop, pop, boom of a rifle range. I hope you won't encounter too many of the sights and sounds of civilization at the campgrounds listed in this book. An equally important factor for me on the beauty scale is the condition of the campground itself and to what extent it has been left in its natural state. Beauty also, of course, takes into consideration any fabulous views of mountains, water, or other natural phenomena.

Site privacy

No one who enjoys the simplicity of tent camping wants to be walled in on all sides by RVs the size of tractor trailers. This category goes hand in hand with the previous one because part of the beauty of a campsite has to do with the privacy of its surroundings. If you've ever crawled out of your tent to embrace a stunning summer morning in you skivvies and found several pairs of very curious eyes staring at you from the neighbor's picture window, you'll know what I mean. I look for campsites that are graciously spaced with lots of heavy foliage in between. You usually have to drive a little deeper into the campground complex for these.

Site spaciousness

This is the category you toss the coin on—and keep your fingers crossed. I'm not as much of a stickler for this category because I'm happy if there's room to park the car off the main campground road, enough space to pitch a two- or four-man tent in a reasonably flat and dry spot, a picnic table for meal

preparation, and a fire pit safely away from the tenting area. At most campgrounds, site spaciousness is sacrificed for site privacy and vice versa. Sometimes you get extremely lucky and have both. Don't be greedy.

Quiet

Again, this category goes along with the beauty of a place. When I go camping, I want to hear the sounds of nature. You know, birds chirping, the wind sighing, a surf crashing, a brook babbling. That kind of stuff. It's not always possible to control the noise volume of your fellow campers, so the closer you can get to natural sounds that can drown them out, the better. Actually, when you have a chance to listen to the quiet of nature, you'll find that it is really rather noisy. But what a lovely cacophony!

Security

Quite a few of the campgrounds in this book are in remote and primitive places without on-site security patrol. In essence, you're on your own. Common sense is a great asset in these cases. Don't leave expensive outdoor gear or valuable camera equipment lying around your campsite or even within view inside your car. If you are at a hosted site, you may feel more comfortable leaving any valuables with them. Or let them know you'll be gone for an extended period so they can keep an eye on your things.

Unfortunately, even in lightly camped areas, vandalism is a common camping problem. In many places, the wild animals can do as much damage as a human being. If you leave food inside your tent or around the campsite, don't be surprised if things look slightly ransacked when you return. The most frequent visitors to food-strewn campsites are birds, squirrels, chipmunks, deer, and bears.

Cleanliness/upkeep

By and large, all the campgrounds in this book rank five stars for this category. I think Washington and Oregon campgrounds are some of the cleanest and tidiest spots I've been in due to the fine management of park and Forest Service attendants. The only time they tend to fall a bit short of expectation is on busy summer weekends. This is usually only in the larger, more developed

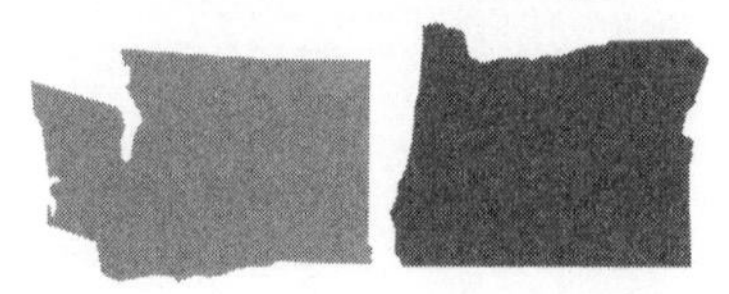

compounds. In more remote areas, the level of cleanliness is most often dependent on the good habits of the campers themselves. Keep that in mind wherever you camp.

Insect control
To my knowledge, spraying for bugs is not a regular practice in Northwest campgrounds. If the campground is situated on a lake (particularly at higher elevations), you can almost bet that mosquitoes will be a nuisance in midsummer. Even if the campground has earned a high insect control rating, it's always a good idea to have a reliable repellent in your cache of camping essentials. Everyone reacts to (and is affected by) the presence of bugs differently. The most common winged critters that cause problems are mosquitoes, no-see-ums, deer flies, sand fleas, and ticks.

Changes
As with any guidebook, changes in the information provided in these listings are inevitable. It's a good idea to call ahead for the most updated report on the campground you've selected. We would appreciate knowing any notable changes that you may come across while using this book.

WASHINGTON CAMPGROUNDS

WESTERN WASHINGTON

BEACON ROCK STATE PARK

Skamania, Washington

The Northwest's longest and largest river cutting a huge sea-level pass through the Cascade Mountains teams with the world's second largest monolith to produce the main attractions for campers at Beacon Rock State Park.

Beacon Rock, once known as Castle Rock, towers 848 feet above the mighty Columbia River in the Columbia River Gorge National Scenic Area and is second only to the Rock of Gibraltar in size. Several other similar but smaller rock formations in this section of the gorge have prompted geologists to hypothesize that Beacon Rock may be the exposed volcanic plug of an ancient mountain, part of a range that preceded the Cascades. The monolith could be as much as nine million years old.

Apparently unimpressed by this massive icon of geologic time, the Army Corps of Engineers wanted to blast Beacon Rock into bits sometime around the turn of the century. Fortunately railroad officials opposed the idea enough to get the demolition stopped. Theirs wasn't a particularly noble reason, however. They just didn't want rocks falling on their new tracks. Another popular idea at the time was to convert the rock to a quarry.

The fate of Beacon Rock remained uncertain until 1915 when Henry Biddle bought it and proceeded to

CAMPGROUND RATINGS

Beauty:	★★★★
Site privacy:	★★★★
Site spaciousness:	★★★★
Quiet:	★★★★★
Security:	★★★★
Cleanliness/upkeep:	★★★★★
Insect control:	★★

Second in size only to the Rock of Gibraltar, Beacon Rock is worth seeing. And Beacon Rock State Park is the camp from which to do it.

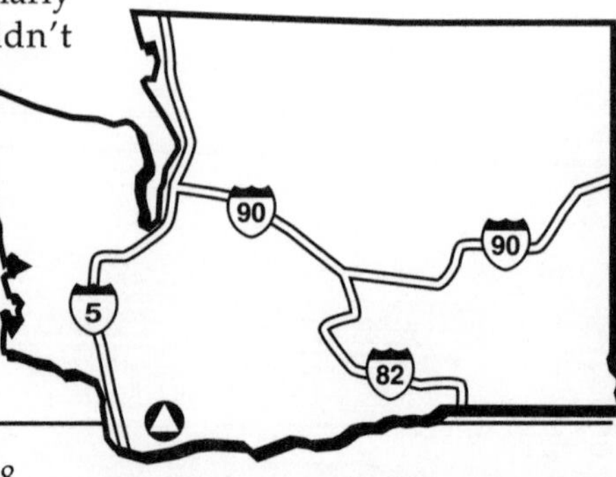

build a trail to its summit. The project cost him $15,000, a considerable sum in those days. When Biddle died, his heirs were instructed to sell Beacon Rock to the State of Washington for a mere dollar. One small restriction accompanied the astonishingly low price, however. The land was to be preserved as a public park.

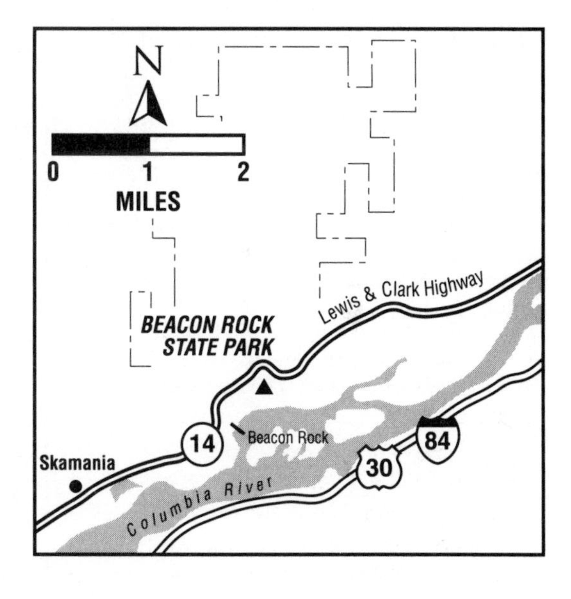

At first the state refused to honor the terms, so the Biddle family approached the State of Oregon with the same deal. An Oregon-owned park on Washington State soil almost became a reality until Washington reconsidered and handed over the buck.

Today the three-quarter mile trail to the top switches back a dizzying 52 times and crosses 22 wooden bridges. Panoramic views up and down the gorge including Oregon's Mount Hood and Washington's Mount Adams are the reward.

Aside from the Beacon Rock trail (which is a must), a network of other paths throughout the park's interior offers destinations to Rodney Falls and Hardy Falls. The Pacific Crest National Scenic Trail intersects the park's trail system at the northeast corner and takes the ambitious wanderer north out of the park and into steep terrain strewn with basaltic rubble to Table Mountain (elevation 1,042 feet). If you follow the Pacific Crest Trail south, you'll come to its crossover point from Oregon at a trailhead near the Bridge of the Gods.

Hamilton Mountain is a more attainable distance for most hikers. At 745 feet, it is the highest point in the park (not including Beacon Rock). Sitting beside the falls as they cascade down Hardy Creek, a forested mountain at your back, watching birds flit and chipmunks scamper and enjoying the fragrant wisps of campfire smoke wafting past are all ingredients for as fine a Northwest outing as anyone could hope for.

The campground is tucked against a forested hillside on the north side of State Route 14. Tent sites are spaced comfortably around the circular paved drive that winds up from the river.

To get there, head east on SR 14 from its junction with I-205 at Ellsworth. The wide expanse of the Columbia is your constant companion as you drive approximately 30 miles on the 2-lane route (Lewis and Clark Highway) to the park's entrance. You'll pass the base of Beacon Rock as you are watching for the signs to the turnoff to the park. Be aware that the road signs around here are a bit confusing and traffic gets congested when motorists slow to gawk at Beacon Rock.

KEY INFORMATION

Beacon Rock State Park
MP3483L, State Route 14
Skamania, WA 98648

Operated by: Washington State Parks and Recreation Commission

Information: (509) 427-8265

Open: April 1 to October

Individual sites: 33 standard, 2 primitive

Each site has: Picnic table, fire grill, shade trees

Site assignment: Reservations for group camping only; otherwise first come, first served

Registration: Self-registration on site

Facilities: Flush toilets, showers (extra fee); firewood (extra fee); playground; dump station; boat dock, rentals, and launch nearby; kitchen; shelter; group overnight facilities; limited disabled access

Parking: At individual sites

Fee: $10 per night; no full hookups

Elevation: 700 feet

Restrictions:

Pets–On leash

Fires–In fire pits only

Alcoholic beverages–Permitted

Vehicles–RVs and trailers up to 50 feet

BECKLER RIVER CAMPGROUND

Skykomish, Washington

You've started the day with a plan to leave Everett in the morning and be in Leavenworth in time for dinner à la campfire. By the time you pack the car, stop off at the great little bakery in Monroe, crawl through Sultan, Startup, and Gold Bar (notorious for their speed traps), gawk at Mount Index, take a short leg-stretching hike to Sunset Falls, stop for lunch at The Bush House in Index, and pause to watch rafters on the Skykomish River from your roadside perch, it's clear that the summer light is fading fast and Leavenworth is still more than an hour away. And you haven't explored Skykomish yet!

Beckler River is one of the few campgrounds along U.S. 2 between Gold Bar and Leavenworth (much of which can be slow going because it is a two-lane road where passing is a suicidal idea). So if you find yourself in need of a quick tent spot, Beckler River Campground serves nicely. Only 60 miles from Seattle, Beckler sits on the banks of the Beckler River 3 miles from the town of Skykomish.

A heavy canopy of western Washington foliage coats the area around the campground as well as the numerous steep-sided river and creek valleys that drain their tributaries into the Beckler River. The moist climate produces tall stands of Douglas fir, western red cedar, oak, maple, and alder. At lower elevations, ferns

CAMPGROUND RATINGS

Beauty:	★★★★★
Site privacy:	★★★
Site spaciousness:	★★★
Quiet:	★★★★
Security:	★★★★★
Cleanliness/upkeep:	★★★★
Insect control:	★★

As a destination campground, Beckler River would probably not make the top of the list. But if you want a good base camp to daytrip into wilderness areas both north and south, enjoy hot springs and historic towns, and hike ridges and run rivers, Beckler is a very good choice.

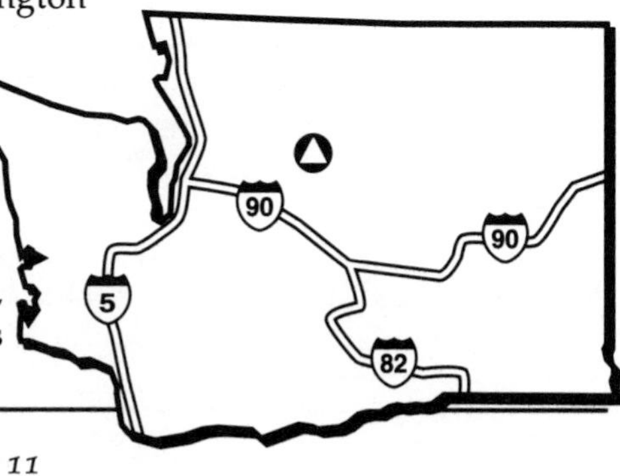

and Oregon grape grow thick, while red and blue huckleberries can be found higher up. It's common to find skunk cabbage and trillium along the riverbeds.

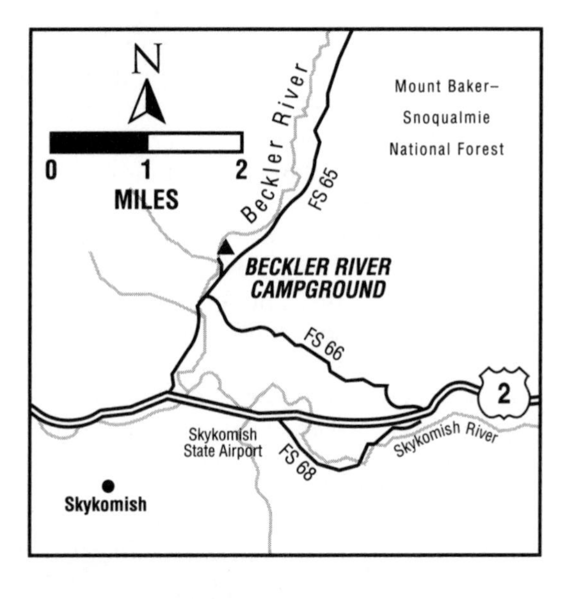

Geologically this area is a wonderment of sharply thrusting young granite pushing up through old, decomposed and metamorphosed material. Estimates date the old rock back as far as 200 million years. An easy place to view this clash of old and ancient is about 3 miles east of Skykomish where the Beckler Peak batholith crosses U.S. 2. This is very close to the Straight Creek fault, which is used by geologists as the official dividing line between the eastern and western slopes of the Cascade Range.

Not far to the east is Stevens Pass, one of the lower passes in the Cascades and a popular ski resort in the wintertime. Once snowmelt clears the trails in summer (usually by mid-July), it is the place to catch the Pacific Crest National Scenic Trail either north or south. East to west, Stevens Pass was once the route of the Great Northern Railway when it was established in the 1890s by James T. Hill. Today the Stevens Pass Historic District preserves what is left of the track and allows visitors to explore along it. A modern railway was built paralleling the old route and has a significance of its own as the longest railroad tunnel (8 miles) in the Western Hemisphere.

Trips into the Beckler backcountry should be prefaced by a visit to the Skykomish Ranger Station. Heavy snow can often keep trails blocked longer than one would imagine. With all the quality mountain terrain to traverse, it will be a temptation to strike out for the nearest ridge.

The Henry M. Jackson Wilderness (named for a former Washington State senator) lies to the north. It has 49 miles of hiking trails that were once the cross-Cascade routes used by early Native Americans and later by exploration teams. Follow the Forest Service road past Garland Hot Springs to reach the trailheads.

To the south is the fabled Alpine Lakes Wilderness, about 300,000 acres that have been the subject of much discussion and debate among outdoor recreation groups and the Forest Service. At this writing, some kind of regulatory system is being considered to reduce the damaging impact of too many people frequenting the fragile lands. Trailheads into Alpine Lakes are just west of Skykomish on Miller River Road, which becomes FS 6412.

To get there, drive 1 mile east of Skykomish on U.S. 2, turn left onto FS 65, and go 2 more miles to the campground.

KEY INFORMATION

Beckler River Campground
c/o Skykomish Ranger District
Box 305
Skykomish, WA 98288

Operated by: Mount Baker-Snoqualmie National Forest

Information: (360) 677-2414

Open: Memorial Day weekend to mid-September

Individual sites: 27

Each site has: Picnic table, fire pit with grill, shade trees, piped water nearby

Site assignment: One-half are first come, first served; one half are reservable; for reservations, call (800) 280-CAMP

Registration: At campground

Facilities: Vault toilets, piped water; firewood; store, ice, laundromat, gas, and 3 cafes within 1 mile; public telephone

Parking: At individual sites

Fee: $10.50 per night

Elevation: 1,000 feet

Restrictions:

Pets–On leash

Fires–In fire pits only

Alcoholic beverages–Permitted

Vehicles–RVs and trailers up to 21 feet

CASCADE ISLANDS CAMPGROUND

Marblemount, Washington

A pleasant streamside setting along one of the myriad tributaries that feed the long and winding Skagit River is the pick for this listing. It is also one that gets overlooked by the hordes of summer vacationers who cram themselves into the precious few campgrounds run by the North Cascades National Park farther up State Route 20 in the Ross Lake National Recreation Area.

Other choices in the immediate vicinity have their limitations—no piped water, private management with an RV orientation, or not enough distance from the beaten track to warrant what I call "getting away from it all."

Cascade Islands is a Department of Natural Resources facility that sits on the shore of the Cascade River about 2 miles upstream from where this characteristic mountain freshet gives over its glacial flow to the Skagit. There is unlikely to be a small river in the entire Cascade Range that is more deserving of its name than the Cascade. Descending as the North Fork from Cascade Peak and combining with generous supplies of melt from Middle Cascade Glacier and South Cascade Glacier to form Middle and South Forks, the Cascade is aptly named. These icy origins do not constitute its entire existence, however. It continues to pick up the offerings of dozens of smaller creeks

CAMPGROUND RATINGS

Beauty:	★★★★
Site privacy:	★★★★
Site spaciousness:	★★★
Quiet:	★★★★★
Security:	★★★
Cleanliness/upkeep:	★★★
Insect control:	★★★

Finding an out-of-the-way campground near the Cascade River is tough, so this one's quiet streamside setting and unlimited hiking options come as a pleasant surprise.

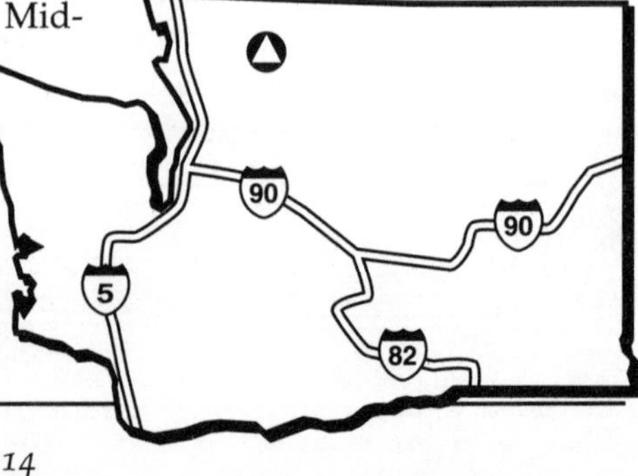

and streams, wending its way north and west along its rather short journey.

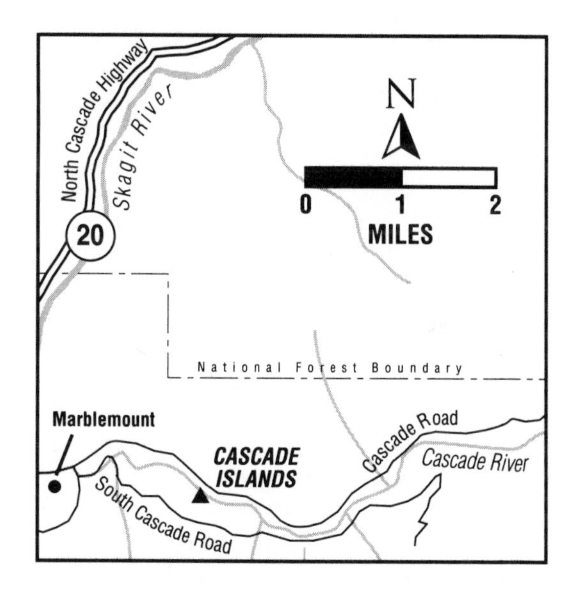

Activities abound within minutes of Cascade Islands. Hiking options are limited only by time and season. To the east and north lies North Cascades National Park with some of the most rugged, demanding terrain in all of Washington. There are views of peaks, glaciers (there are 300 total in the North Cascade Range), waterfalls, meadows, and forested valleys that could easily absorb all of the time you have. South over the ridges from the campground is Glacier Peak Wilderness, another vast expanse of alpine wonderland with 450 miles of trails.

For boaters, two sections of the Skagit offer their own appeal and are part of the river's Wild and Scenic designation. From Newhalem to just above Marblemount is a 10-mile stretch, on what is known as the Upper Skagit, that is a controlled flow. This section is considered Class II and III, depending on water levels. There are several rapids to contend with.

From Marblemount to Rockport (another 10-mile trip), the difficulty level is Class II and suitable for a variety of craft. This section of the river is quite popular year-round. In winter, float trip after float trip takes passengers through the Skagit River Bald Eagle Natural Area to observe hundreds of the national bird in one of its favorite winter feeding grounds.

It is no accident that the eagles have homed in on this section of the Skagit. These are prime steelhead waters as many a fisherman can attest. A trip to the nearby Skagit Hatchery might be in order, if that is your interest.

For information on other opportunities, visit the North Cascades National Park headquarters in Marblemount. Be advised that permits are required for certain backcountry activities within the park.

To get there, take Cascade Road east from Marblemount for two-thirds of a mile, turn right onto Rockport Cascade Road, and then quickly left onto South Cascade Road. The campground is a little more than a mile down South Cascade Road.

KEY INFORMATION

Cascade Islands Campground
c/o Rockport State Park
5051 WA 20
Concrete, WA 98237

Operated by: Rockport State Park

Information: (360) 853-8461

Open: May to October

Individual sites: 15

Each site has: Picnic tables, fire grill, tent pads

Site assignment: First come, first served; no reservations

Registration: Not necessary

Facilities: Piped water, vault toilets; firewood; store and cafe within 1 mile (in Marblemount); more services and a cafe a few miles west on State Route 20 (in Rockport)

Parking: At individual sites

Fee: No fee

Elevation: 1,000 feet

Restrictions:

Pets–On leash

Fires–In fire pits only

Alcoholic beverages–Permitted

Vehicles–Small, self-contained RVs; no hookups

Other–Permits required for some backcountry activities

CORRAL PASS CAMPGROUND

Near Crystal Mountain Ski Area, Washington

For your own personal, unsurpassed view of the north face of Mount Rainier and for a different perspective of Crystal Mountain Ski Area, take a hard left off State Route 410 about 30 miles out of Enumclaw onto Forest Service Road 7174. This is a challenging piece of roadway that is marked by a sign for a campground at the entrance.

The bumper-to-bumper traffic will go whizzing by, and you'll find yourself facing nearly 6 miles of a steep, winding dirt route that's best traveled by high-clearance vehicles. Trust me. It will be worth the effort once you reach the campground.

But first, do you have water with you? If not, remedy that situation now. There are a few small creeks that trickle off the sides of Mutton Mountain and Castle Mountain, but these can be unreliable in late summer or during an unusually dry season. There is no piped water at Corral Pass.

Due to its high altitude and possible heavy snowfalls in winter, this National Forest–managed campground has a relatively short usage period—between July and late September. This is an area of unpredictable weather patterns ruled by that giant white snowcone to the south known by locals as "the Mountain" and by the rest of the world as Mount Rainier. Thun-

CAMPGROUND RATINGS

Beauty:	★★★★
Site privacy:	★★★★★
Site spaciousness:	★★★★★
Quiet:	★★★★★
Security:	★★
Cleanliness/upkeep:	★★★
Insect control:	★★★

Prepare for six miles of steep, winding dirt road. Your reward? Your own private, incredible view of Mount Rainier.

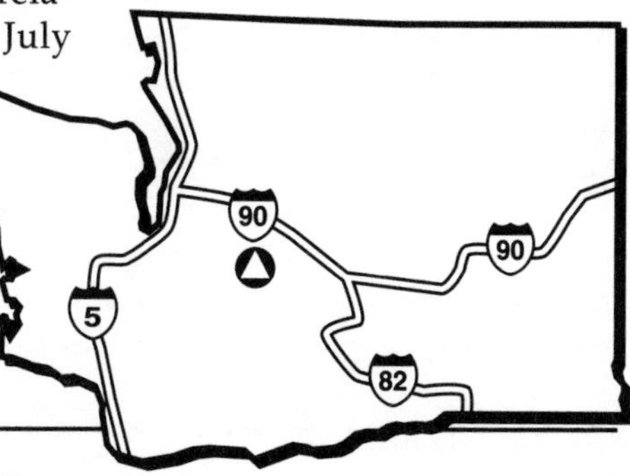

derstorms can pop up in a flash as cool, moist, western clouds clash with warm, uplifting breezes on the eastern slopes. Corral Pass sits nearly on the Cascade spine and gets direct hits of these conditions as they make their transitions literally overhead.

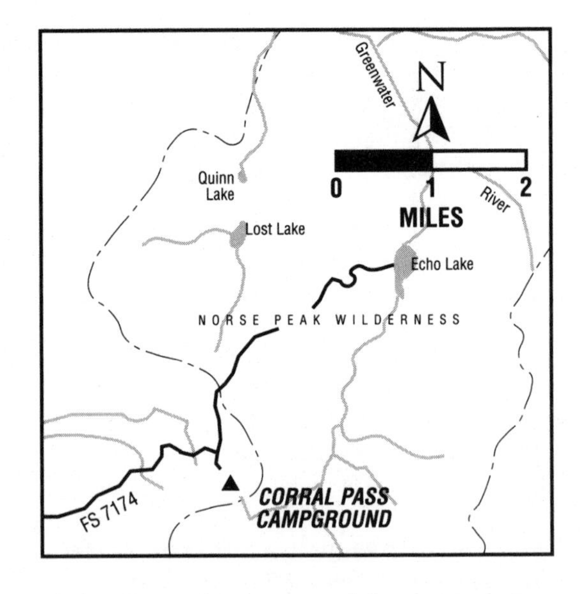

Crystal Mountain Ski Area takes full advantage of this unique situation in winter. That time of year, the warm and wet western air nudges up against a cold, eastern wall, dumping moisture in soft, dry, white accumulations that make Crystal the choice for steep and deep over other Washington ski resorts.

Hopefully you've come to Corral Pass for the backcountry hiking options, which I am happy to report are plentiful. For starters, there's Norse Peak Wilderness brushing the ridge top just east of the campground and covering more than 50,000 acres of diverse terrain dissected by 52 miles of hiking trails. There is a surprising variety of wildlife and vegetation to enjoy as well. Mountain goats, elk, and deer, to name a few. The wildflowers in the meadows around Noble Knob are known to rival those at Paradise on Mount Rainier's southern slope when they are in full bloom (late June to early August, depending on the elevation). Berry-picking is prime in late August and early September.

A long hike that includes a bit of history and requires an overnight stay at one of several campsites along the way is the Echo Lake/Greenwater River trail. Near the Greenwater end of the trailhead is Naches Trail, the route first used by several wagon train parties in 1853. Most of the original route has long been obscured by motorbikes and jeeps allowed in the area, but the still-famous "Cliff," where the pioneers lowered their wagons and horses on ropes, can be appreciated by a hike down it.

Spur trails leading from Echo Lake (elevation 3,819 feet) also continue north and south to points along the Pacific Crest National Scenic Trail. From Corral Pass, a trail south stays within Norse Peak Wilderness the entire way until it hooks up with Pacific Crest Trail at a spot known as Little Crow Basin (about 4 miles). Several miles farther along the Pacific Crest Trail is Big Crow Basin and views down to Crystal Mountain Ski Area. This is probably the turnaround point if you're just out for the day. Retrace your steps to Corral Pass, enjoying vistas both east and west.

To get there, from Enumclaw (roughly 40 miles southeast of Seattle) take SR 410 southeast for about 30 miles. Turn left onto FS 7174 and follow it to its end (6 miles). The highway marker for FS 7174 can be obscured by overhanging foliage, so keep a sharp lookout for it on the right side of the road. If you find yourself at the turnoff to Crystal Mountain Ski Area and the entrance to Mount Rainier National Park, you've gone about a mile too far.

KEY INFORMATION

Corral Pass Campground
c/o White River Ranger District
Enumclaw, WA 98022

Operated by: Mount Baker-Snoqualmie National Forest

Information: (360) 825-6585

Open: July to late September

Individual sites: 26; tents only

Each site has: Picnic table, fire grill

Site assignment: First come, first served; no reservations

Registration: Not necessary

Facilities: Vault toilets, firewood, horse trailer loading ramp

Parking: At individual sites

Fee: No fee

Elevation: 5,600 feet

Restrictions:

Pets–On leash

Fires–In fire pits only

Alcoholic beverages–Permitted

Vehicles–RVs and trailers not recommended on the steep, rough road

Other–No piped water

DASH POINT STATE PARK

Federal Way, Washington

Located on the shore of Puget Sound only 6 miles north of Tacoma and 20 miles south of Seattle, Dash Point State Park is 400 acres of lush privacy complemented by modern facilities including hot showers and flush toilets, dump station, and hookup services. Tent sites sit under the protection of huge moss-covered maples that tower over an assortment of western Washington foliage—alder, hemlock, salmonberry, salal, and huckleberry. Sword ferns as tall as three feet thrive in the damp, shrouded climes. Madrona trees, barely clinging to the steep and crumbling cliffs above the beach, provide peekaboo views through the thick understory with their signature peeling red bark, gnarled limbs, and dark-green, all-season leaves. Dogwood trees dress things up in spring with fresh, white blossoms—a stark contrast to all that is green, green, green.

Beachside, Dash Point is one of the few parks south of Seattle that actually has sand to wiggle your toes in. Thanks to a 1% slope, roughly 2,200 feet extend out into Puget Sound, warming the shallow waters that pass over it and making Dash Point a prized swimming area. (For the uninformed, Puget Sound temperatures remain fairly constant year-round in the numbing 40s and 50s.) Puget Sound is saltwater, by the way.

CAMPGROUND RATINGS

Beauty:	★★★★★
Site privacy:	★★★★
Site spaciousness:	★★★★
Quiet:	★★★
Security:	★★★
Cleanliness/upkeep:	★★★★
Insect control:	N/A

If you've just flown in to the Seattle/Tacoma area with your backpack, campstove, and tent roll waiting in the baggage claim and you want to make a quick escape, relief is just moments away.

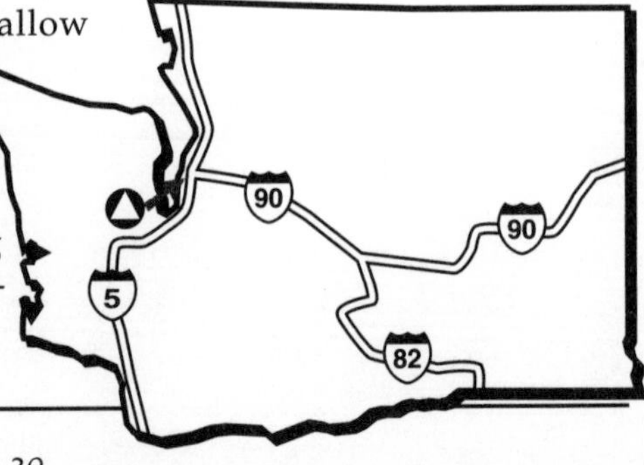

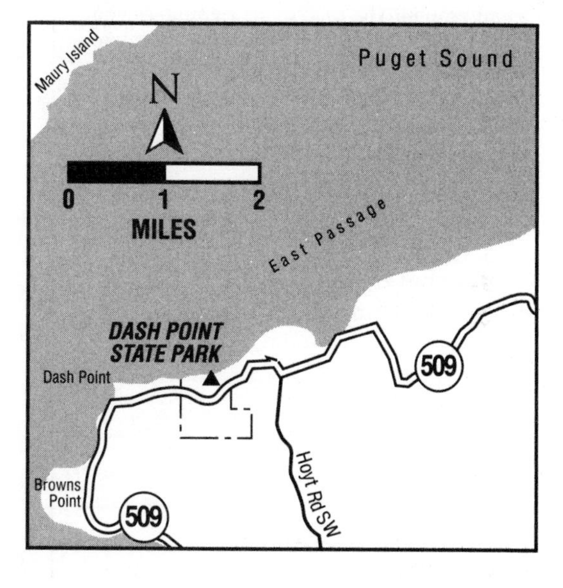

You may want to lay out a summer supper on one of the many picnic tables down by the shoreline and let your mind drift back to an earlier time in Puget Sound history.

In the year 1792, Captain George Vancouver and his crew found their way along this uncharted inland body of water. On May 26, the explorers stopped for dinner at Browns Point (the next point south toward Tacoma) and, in the fading twilight, enjoyed the views of the Olympic Mountains and Vashon Island. Modern-day picnickers can admire similar scenes but with the glare of distant city lights diluting the glow of spectacular sunsets. In summer, sunsets in the Northwest can linger as late as 11 p.m.

The park is open all year, and spaces fill up fast in the summertime, especially from Thursday through Sunday. Overnighters passing through on the "I-5 corridor" give the park plenty of use.

If you have time for metropolitan attractions, both Seattle and Tacoma have their share. The Pike Place Market, the Seattle Center with its landmark Space Needle, Pioneer Square, waterfront shops and eateries, the much-talked-about SAM (Seattle Art Museum), and interesting neighborhoods bordering downtown—all are part of the flavor and excitement of Seattle. Tacoma is home to the Washington State Historical Society Museum, the distinctive Tacoma Art Museum, Point Defiance Park, Zoo, and Aquarium, and the Pantages theater. You'll also find a revitalized urban center, lively Old Town and waterfront scenes, with restaurants, taverns, shops, two fishing piers, and a paved walkway.

To get there, from Seattle take the 320th Street exit off I-5 at Federal Way, and head west to 21st Avenue Southwest. Turn right, and then turn left at the intersection of SR 509 (Marine View Drive). The park entrance is about 3 miles south on SR 509. Turn left for the campground. The road to the right takes you down to the parking area and the pathway to the beach.

KEY INFORMATION

Dash Point State Park
5700 Southwest Dash Point Road
Federal Way, WA 98003

Information: (206) 593-2206

Open: All year, with limited winter access

Individual sites: 138

Each site has: Picnic table, fire pit with grill, piped water, shade trees

Site assignment: Reservations accepted, call (800) 233-0321 (fills up quickly Thursday through Sunday during summer); $6 fee for reservations

Registration: At camp office

Facilities: Bathhouse with sinks, flush toilets, showers, and hot water; public telephone; boat put-in; play area; group camp; swimming beach; picnic area; amphitheater

Parking: At individual sites

Fee: $10 per night, basic tent camper; $15 full electric hookup

Elevation: Sea level

Restrictions:

Pets–On leash

Fires–In fire pits only

Alcoholic beverages–Prohibited

Vehicles–RVs and trailers up to 35 feet

Other–10-day limit on length of stay, May to September 30; 15-day limit, October to April 30

DOSEWALLIPS CAMPGROUND

Brinnon, Washington

Pick a valley. Any valley. It's hard to make a bad choice when it comes to the options in Olympic National Park.

One of my favorites is the Dosewallips River Valley, which looks relatively unchanged since the days of its settlement in the 1860s. Picture-perfect farmhouses, neatly painted white, occupy the lowlands that were cleared to provide room for gardens and orchards. In addition to the fertile soil, early settlers soon discovered the bounty of Hood Canal, with its fish, clams, crabs, oysters, shrimp, and the oddball geoduck (pronounced *gooey duck*). The shellfish industry today suffers an uneven existence due largely to pollution of inland waters, but the geoduck, a member of the clam family, survives against all odds. In 1992, a four-pound monster was hauled from its salty habitat.

Settlement around the Brinnon area developed mainly out of the expectation that a rail line to Portland would create a booming logging industry. Well, the railway never materialized, but a mill and hotel did. Logging continues today, although the main sources of income for Olympic Peninsula residents are tied to recreation.

As you make your way along Forest Service Road 2610 toward the campground, the elevation gain is slow but steady, following the

CAMPGROUND RATINGS

Beauty:	★★★★★
Site privacy:	★★
Site spaciousness:	★★★
Quiet:	★★★★
Security:	★★★★
Cleanliness/upkeep:	★★★★
Insect control:	N/A

A major trailhead into the Olympic National Park interior, located in the picturesque Dosewallips River Valley.

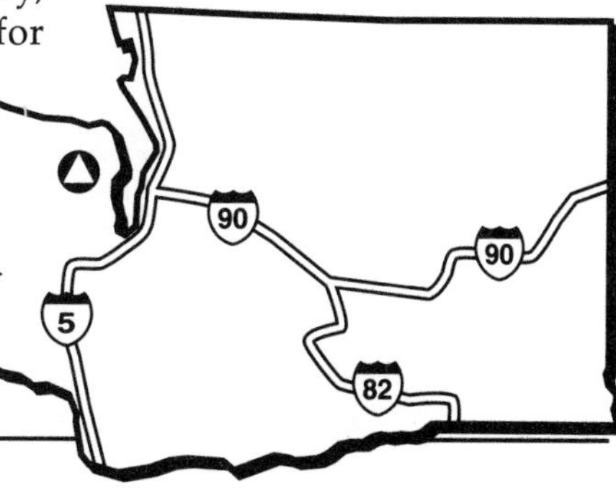

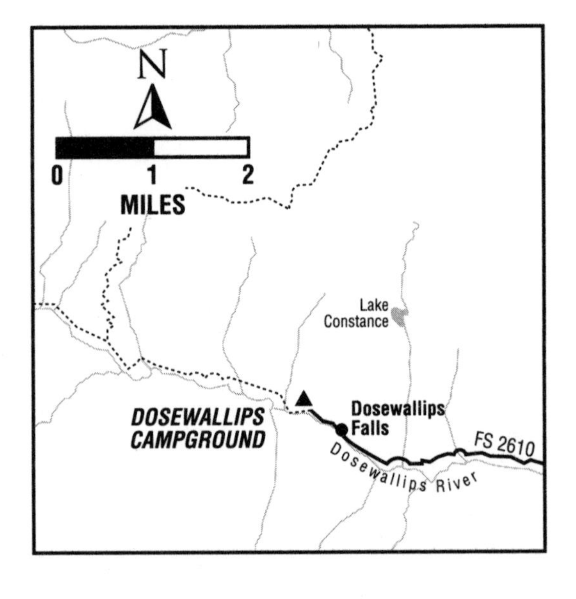

glaciated waters of the Dosewallips River all the way.

Views of the broad, endless, U-shapedvalley appear at various rises, falls, and curves of the road, building anticipation for the lovely hiking opportunities that await the foot traveler. If you haven't already used up all of your excess time by stopping for photos of the river along the way (which you'll be easily tempted to do), stop at Elkhorn Campground for a picnic. This less remote option to Dosewallips Campground sits on the northern edge of The Brothers Wilderness boundary about 12 miles in. It's an excellent spot to regroup for the final 3 miles up to Dosewallips. There is riverside access here for a pleasant break among towering conifers and a thick array of mosses, ferns, rhododendron, and salal.

By this time, the road has switched from pavement to all-weather gravel, but the last few miles will still challenge the best of them. One section paralleling the steep drop of Dosewallips Falls goes nearly straight up and is pocked with potholes and sharp rocks. This is where the RVs wish they had stayed at Elkhorn. Another spot is quite narrow, crossing a cascading creek just after rounding a hairpin turn. Drive slowly, and keep a sharp lookout for oncoming cars. It's easy to be surprised by them both in the gloom and the dappled sunlight, if you are lucky enough to have the latter.

Since this is a major trailhead into the Olympic National Park interior, most of your fellow campers are probably readying themselves for an extended outing, as you may well be doing yourself. There is a ranger station up the hill to the right of the parking lot that is staffed from May through the middle of October. You may want to check on current trail conditions and any other useful information that will make your trip as enjoyable as possible. This is a national park, after all, so what you're used to in national forests or wilderness areas may not apply. You can also pick up trail guides and maps of the park at the station.

As far as supplies go, don't expect a national park concession stand at the end of the road. Stock up in Brinnon or wherever your trip originates.

A Gore-Tex rainsuit could be your most cherished piece of clothing in the Dosewallips Valley because wet, mild weather predominates most of the year. The higher you go, the cooler but not necessarily drier things become. Up to 140 inches of precipitation have been measured in parts of the park. That translates to heavy snow on the high trails and passes. "Indian summer" may be the best time to visit.

To get there, take U.S. 101 to Brinnon, and then take FS 2610 west for about 15 miles. The Dosewallips Campground is located at the end of FS 2610 (Dosewallips River Road).

KEY INFORMATION

Dosewallips Campground
c/o Olympic National Park
P.O. Box 197
Brinnon, WA 98548

Operated by: Olympic National Park

Information: (360) 452-4501

Open: Third week of April through October 15, depending on weather

Individual sites: 32

Each site has: Picnic table, fire pit with grill, piped water, shade trees

Site assignment: First come, first served; no reservations

Registration: Self-registration on site

Facilities: Bathhouse with flush toilets, disabled access, and running water

Parking: At individual sites

Fee: $8 per night

Elevation: 1,540 feet

Restrictions:

Pets–On leash

Fires–In fire pits only

Alcoholic beverages–Permitted

Vehicles–No accommodations for RVs or trailers

DUNGENESS RECREATION AREA

Sequim, Washington

Let me tell you about the day I almost didn't discover the rare beauty of Dungeness Recreation Area.

It was a hot and windy summer weekend sometime back in the late 1970s. A friend and I had a late-afternoon, last-minute wild hair to hop a ferry across Puget Sound and take our bicycles with us. Destination: Dungeness Spit. We had been told that this was a special and unusual place, and we were eager to see firsthand if the description was deserving.

By mid-morning the next day, we found the park entrance and started down the gravel road, following signs to the trailhead. Suddenly an enormous luxury automobile careened toward us, filling every usable inch of the lane and throwing up a shower of stones and dust behind it. The car ground noisily (but harmlessly) to a halt only inches away from us. A voice growled, "No sense goin' down there. Don't know what all the fuss is about."

Once we got over the initial shock of the encounter, we proceeded to ignore the eloquent advice of this rugged outdoorsman and made a beeline through the woods to one of the supreme natural wonders of Washington State.

Dungeness Spit, the main attraction in the Dungeness Recreation Area/National Wildlife Refuge con-

CAMPGROUND RATINGS

Beauty:	★★★★★
Site privacy:	★★★★★
Site spaciousness:	★★★★
Quiet:	★★★★
Security:	★★★★
Cleanliness/upkeep:	★★★★
Insect control:	★★★

This is the place from which to explore Dungeness Spit, one of the supreme natural wonders of Washington State.

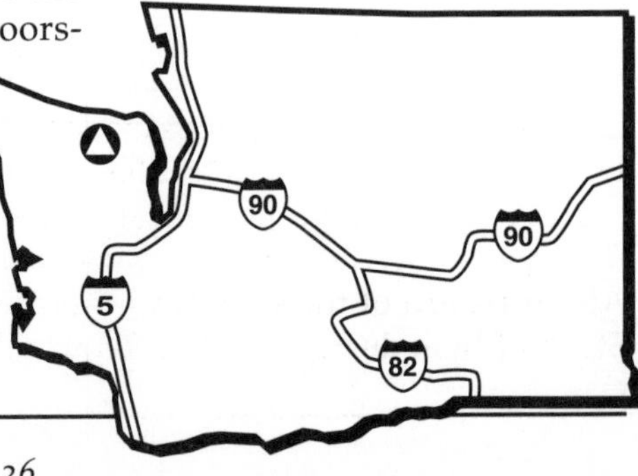

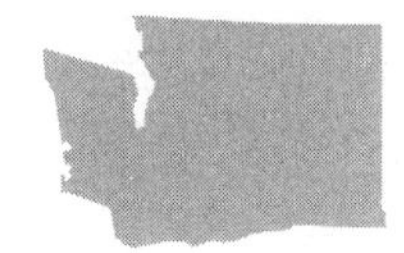

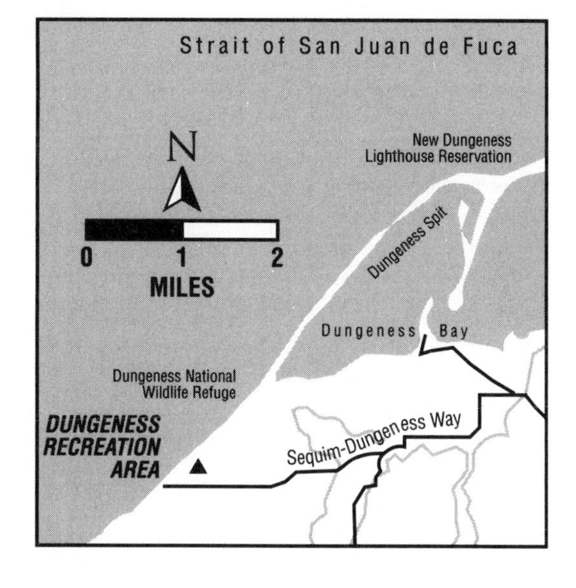

glomerate, is the longest natural sand spit in the United States. Arching nearly 7 miles into the Strait of Juan de Fuca on the Olympic Peninsula, this unique landform averages only 100 yards wide for its entire length. Its outer (western) shore faces the open surf and uninterrupted winds of the strait, causing driftwood to collect in jumbled masses like piles of giant discarded bones.

The inner shore—with smaller Graveyard Spit protruding from it—marks the boundary of Dungeness Bay. The innermost shoreline of this bay—actually an extremely shallow lagoon formed by Graveyard's finger—beckons thousands of migratory and wintering shorebirds that rest on the lush vegetation that flourishes in these marshlike conditions. The oldest inland lighthouse in Washington sits a half-mile from the spit's end and warns off passing ships that can easily miscalculate their distance from barely submerged shoals.

The entire expanse of spits, tidelands, wetlands, landmarks, and adjoining surf forms Dungeness National Wildlife Refuge. While jurisdiction of the refuge belongs to the U.S. Department of Fish and Wildlife, Dungeness Recreation Area is in the hands of the Clallam County Parks Department. It is the largest of nine facilities managed by the county agency, most of which make use of the saltwater northern peninsula shore in some fashion.

The Dungeness Recreation Area campsites are well-designed around two loops, affording ultimate privacy with dense undergrowth between sites. About a third of the sites are spaced along a high bluff that overlooks the Strait of Juan de Fuca with million-dollar views. On a clear night, look for the twinkling lights of Victoria, British Columbia's capital, on the tip of Vancouver Island. If you can tear yourself away from the view, treat yourself to dinner at the legendary Three Crabs Restaurant in Dungeness, and then drowse by a blazing fire back at your campsite.

You will be pleasantly surprised to learn that Dungeness Recreation Area lies within the rain shadow of the Olympic Mountains. As a result, it receives an average of only 15 inches of rain per year.

Despite the moderate year-round climate, the campground is open only from February 1 to October 1. Summer can be quite busy, so you may want to try the off-season.

In addition to the ever-popular beachcombing, other activities in the park include horseback riding (separate equestrian trail and unloading area), gamebird hunting in designated areas, and good old-fashioned picnicking on the picnic tables along the million-dollar-view bluff.

To get there from Sequim (17 miles east of Port Angeles), drive 5 miles west on U.S. 101 to Kitchen-Dick Lane. Turn north, and drive 3 miles, watching for signs to the recreation area campground and entrance.

KEY INFORMATION

Dungeness Recreation Area
223 East 4th Street
Port Angeles, WA 98362

Operated by: Clallam County Parks Department

Information: (360) 683-5847

Open: February 1 to October 1

Individual sites: 65

Each site has: Picnic table, fire pit, shade trees

Site assignment: First come, first served; no reservations

Registration: At park information booth from daylight to dusk

Facilities: Bathhouse with sinks, toilets, showers, hot water; public telephone; playground; firewood (for a small fee)

Parking: At individual sites

Fee: $10 per night

Elevation: Sea level

Restrictions:

Pets–On leash, no dogs on beach

Fires–In fire pits only

Alcoholic beverages–Prohibited

Vehicles–No limit on RV or trailer size

EVERGREEN COURT CAMPGROUND

Ocean Park, Washington

Long Beach Peninsula, so named by its claim to be the world's longest beach, struggles to find a workable balance between such opposing forces as tourism promoters, real estate developers, oyster farmers, birdwatchers, cranberry harvesters, and fishermen. In the midst of this multiple-use stretch of surf and sand is Evergreen Court Campground, a five-acre haven for those willing to make the circuitous journey to this place of subtle beauty. Its proximity to Leadbetter Point State Park on Willapa Bay and the 11,000-acre Willapa National Wildlife Refuge (sharing Leadbetter Point, about 10 miles north) makes Evergreen Court the perfect choice for those interested in all that these state- and federal-managed areas offer.

For ocean access, Klipsan Beach trail can be found about a half mile north of the campground. A place to clean fish is provided for those who have a bit of luck at freshwater Loomis Lake, which is connected to the campground by a slough. Although the resort is not the exclusive domain of tent campers—it's tough finding one on the peninsula that is—manager Patty Noyes assures that there is a distinct "illusion of isolation." Woods of shore pines help create this atmosphere. Two miles up the road, the illusion becomes one of civilization in the small town of

CAMPGROUND RATINGS

Beauty:	★★★
Site privacy:	★★★
Site spaciousness:	★★★
Quiet:	★★★★
Security:	★★★★★
Cleanliness/upkeep:	★★★★★
Insect control:	★★★★

This is the only substantial tent-camping option on the north end of Long Beach Peninsula.

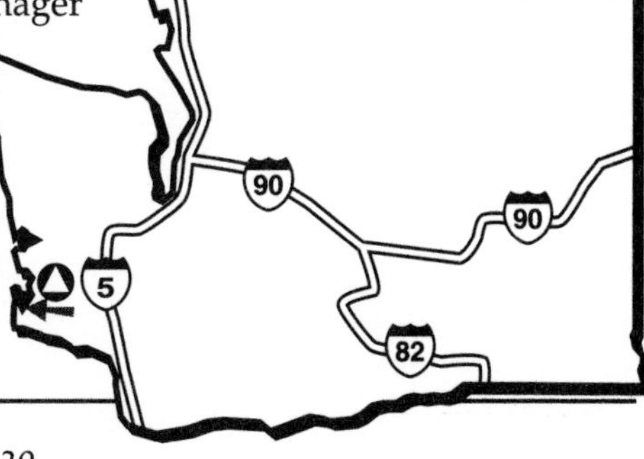

Ocean Park. The basics are here—store, cafe, and laundromat.

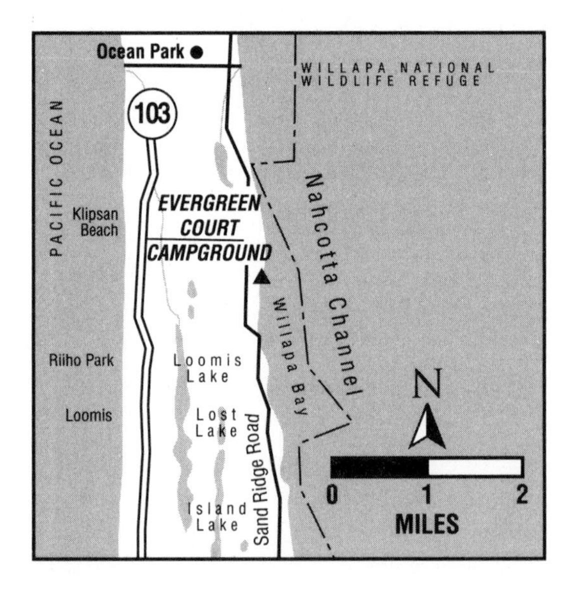

The weather on this coastal finger of land is relatively unchanging throughout the year. The moderate winter climate is good news for birdwatchers because winter can be one of the best times to visit Willapa National Wildlife Refuge. Bring your binoculars and brandy to view the several hundred species of migratory waterfowl and shorebirds that find this temperate sanctuary to be their version of the Mexican Riviera. Spring and fall are good times, too, because the birds are on the move to and from their winter quarters.

Another good reason to come during the off-season is that a sizable portion of Leadbetter Point is closed to human access from April to August to ensure that the nesting snowy plover remains undisturbed. Trails throughout Leadbetter and the refuge are marked, winding through shore pines and sand dunes.

The Long Island unit of Willapa National Wildlife Refuge has its own appeal but requires a little more effort to enjoy properly. This is the largest estuarine island along the Pacific Coast and is accessible only by boat. Launch your sea kayak from the put-in on U.S. 101, about 2 miles south of the Naselle River crossing, and head across the narrow channel. Trails on the island are actually abandoned logging roads dating from the 1940s and 1950s, but nature has done an admirable job of reducing them to mere footpaths. Active logging roads do exist, however. In a land-use exchange program with the U.S. Department of Fish and Wildlife, Weyerhauser Corporation has the go-ahead to log second-growth forests until 1995. The exchange requires that 274 acres of old growth remain intact.

If you're in a mood to play tourist, visit historic Oysterville or indulge yourself in an exquisite meal at the Ark in Nahcotta. A worthy side trip at the southern end of the peninsula is the Lewis and Clark Interpretive Center, overlooking the mouth of the mighty Columbia River. Cape Disappointment and North Head lighthouses, which flank the southern tip of the peninsula, are two of the oldest on the West Coast.

To get there from Seattle, take I-5 to Kelso/Longview (133 miles). Go west on SR 4 for 62 miles to Johnson's Landing. Turn south onto U.S. 101 across the Naselle River and around the southern end of Willapa Bay to the turnoff for SR 103 and Long Beach Peninsula. Take SR 103 north. Evergreen Court Campground is 7 miles north of Long Beach at the intersection of SR 103 and 222nd Avenue.

To get there from Portland, take U.S. 30 northwest along the Columbia River for 95 miles to Astoria. Cross the bridge into Washington on U.S. 101, turning left (west) onto SR 103 after 10 miles. From there, the directions are the same as from Seattle.

KEY INFORMATION

Evergreen Court Campground
222nd Avenue and State Route 103
P.O. Box 488
Ocean Park, WA 98640

Operated by: Murl Noyes

Information: (360) 665-6351

Open: All year

Individual sites: 8

Each site has: Picnic table, fire pit with grill

Site assignment: Reservations recommended in summer; first come, first served in off-season

Registration: At campground office or by mail with deposit

Facilities: Bathhouse with sinks, toilets, showers, hot water; playground

Parking: At individual sites or in main parking lot

Fee: $9 per night for 2 people; $1 each additional person

Elevation: Sea level

Restrictions:

Pets–On leash

Fires–In fire pits only

Alcoholic beverages–Permitted

Vehicles–Separate area with hookups for RVs

FORT EBEY STATE PARK

Coupeville, Washington

Situated in relatively underdeveloped waterfront beauty, Fort Ebey is increasingly popular among tent campers and others looking to escape urban life. The fort itself was one of four artillery forts established by the military in 1942 to defend the state during World War II. The other three (Forts Casey, Flagler, and Worden) also occupy choice waterfront real estate on either side of Admiralty Inlet, joining Ebey in guarding the mouth of Puget Sound today as historic state parks.

From a tent camping perspective, Fort Ebey—named for the pioneering Isaac Ebey family that settled the area—is decidedly the least developed. It is evident that every attempt has been made to retain the natural beauty of the area. Old-growth Douglas fir marks this region, which escaped the usual total desecration by logging interests. An undergrowth of salal, huckleberry, Scotch broom, and rhododendron isn't dense but provides pleasant greenbelts between campsites. In mid-spring, the wild rhododendron fill the park with a profusion of large, colorful blossoms.

It is worth noting that the park attendants have been known to turn away as many as 200 cars per day during heavy summer usage.

CAMPGROUND RATINGS

Beauty:	★★★★★
Site privacy:	★★★
Site spaciousness:	★★★★
Quiet:	★★★
Security:	★★★★★
Cleanliness/upkeep:	★★★★
Insect control:	★★

Hop a ferryboat—preferably the one that leaves from Mukilteo, south of Everett—and head for the westernmost tip of Whidbey Island to enjoy the camping delights of one of Washington's newest state parks.

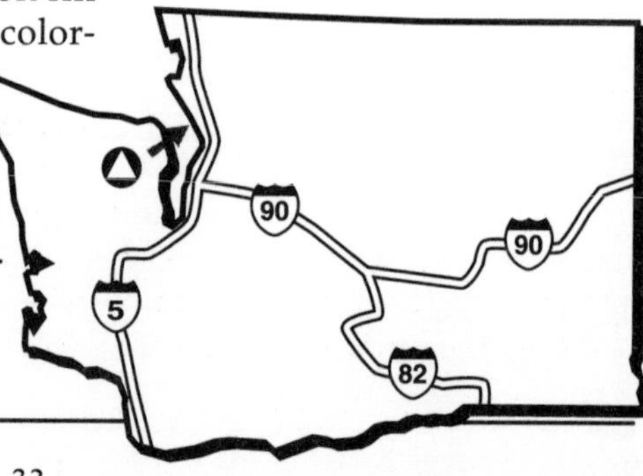

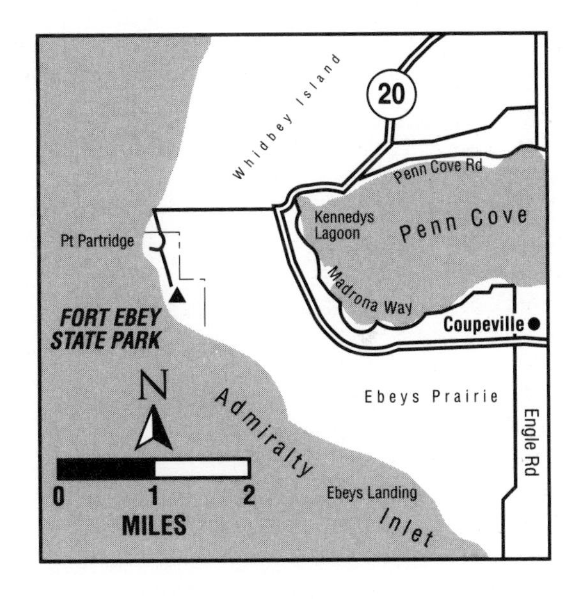

Since the park is now open all year, you may want to miss the crowds and take an equally enjoyable weekend retreat in the off-season.

This area of western Washington tends to be less rainy than other parts since it is influenced by the "rain shadow" phenomenon of the Olympic Mountains to the west. The weather, however, wreaks havoc on the place regularly. It may be drier at Fort Ebey but it is not necessarily tamer. The park faces west onto the Strait of Juan de Fuca and is buffeted constantly by winds funneling in from the Pacific Ocean.

The delicate composition of glacial debris—sand and gravel—that makes up Whidbey Island is often no match for the howling furies that descend. Point Partridge, which I remember as a high, grassy bluff not more than 15 years ago, has been gnawed and clawed beyond recognition by the vengeance of seasonal storms. More than 2,000 of the majestic old-growth firs gracing the park grounds toppled like matchsticks in the fierce snow and windstorm of December 1990. Cleanup teams are still trying to deal with the massive pieces of timber.

There are plenty of activities within the 226-acre park. Beachcombing along the driftwood-laden shoreline. Hiking the wooded trails along the bluffline. Fishing for bass in freshwater Lake Pondilla. Watching a surprising variety of wildlife, including bald eagles, deer, geese, ducks, raccoons, rabbits, pheasant, and grouse. Seeking out the varieties of cactus (yes, cactus!) that grow in this unusual "banana belt" region of western Washington. Exploring the fort's old gun emplacements.

If this doesn't satisfy you, numerous attractions in Coupeville and Oak Harbor should suffice. There are several other state parks in the neighborhood, too. Of particular note is Fort Casey, which has an interpretive center and Admiralty Head Lighthouse. Ebeys Landing National Historic Reserve preserves the legacy of the early pioneers.

To get there from Seattle, drive north on I-5 and State Routes 526 and 525 to Mukilteo and the Washington State Ferry terminal for Whidbey Island. Once on the island, follow SR 525 north, pick up U.S. 20 at Keystone, and continue north to Libbey Road and signs to the park. Total driving distance on Whidbey Island is about 35 miles.

An alternative route is to take U.S. 20 west from I-5 at Burlington (just over 60 miles north of Seattle), and drive down the northern half of Whidbey Island through scenic Deception Pass. This route allows you to avoid ferry lines.

KEY INFORMATION

Fort Ebey State Park
North Fort Ebey Road
Coupeville, WA 98239

Operated by: Washington State Parks and Recreation Commission

Information: (360) 678-4636

Open: Late February to October 31

Individual sites: 53

Each site has: Picnic table, fire grill, shade trees

Site assignment: First come, first served; reservations accepted, call (800) 452-5687, $6 fee

Registration: At campground office

Facilities: Bathhouse with sinks, toilets, showers, hot water; public telephone; boat put-in on lake; picnic area; disabled access

Parking: At individual sites

Fee: $11 per night

Elevation: Sea level

Restrictions:

Pets–On leash

Fires–In fire pits only

Alcoholic beverages–Permitted

Vehicles–No accommodations for RVs or trailers

HOH RAIN FOREST CAMPGROUND

Olympic National Park, Washington

The first thing you'll notice as you're driving up Hoh River Road toward the Hoh Rain Forest Visitor Center and Campground is just how green everything is around you. Even the brief bits of sun that manage to leak through the nearly impenetrable canopy of foliage seem to have a green tinge.

The second thing you'll notice is the pale gray-green shrouds of mosses and lichens that drape ghoulishly from tree branches. The weight of these hangers-on often causes limbs to snap under the stress.

Third, as you stand amidst the hushed majesty of this primeval forest , you'll notice the most insidious yet perpetual characteristic of a temperate rain forest—the steady plink! plink! plink! as droplet after droplet of moisture makes its small but significant contribution to this fascinating, self-sustaining ecosystem.

The Hoh Rain Forest is only one of three temperate rain forests in the entire world. It has had the good fortune to remain in its original state for thousands of years, thanks to the vision of a few men around the turn of the century who recommended the preservation of the Roosevelt elk habitat. Their efforts led first to the creation of the Olympic Forest Reserve, then under Teddy Roosevelt to Mount Olympus

CAMPGROUND RATINGS

Beauty:	★★★★★
Site privacy:	★★★★
Site spaciousness:	★★★★
Quiet:	★★★★
Security:	★★★
Cleanliness/upkeep:	★★★★★
Insect control:	★★★★★

One of only three temperate rain forests in the world, this is a unique and therefore popular destination, especially with hikers. You may want to visit in the off-season.

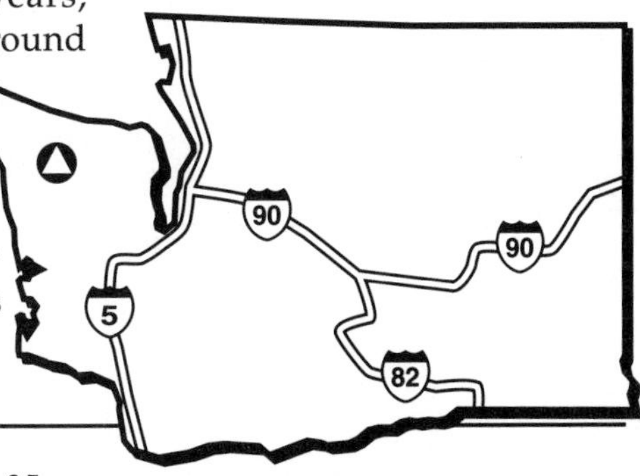

National Monument, and finally under Franklin Roosevelt, to Olympic National Park.

You will notice as you make your way around Olympic Peninsula to the Hoh entrance that logging has been rampant up to the park boundary. Examples of the colossal trees that once blanketed the western slopes of the Olympic Mountains all the way to the coast have, fortunately, been preserved within the park's borders. Four of the nine world record holders are along the Hoh River and its forks. Check with the visitor center for their exact locations.

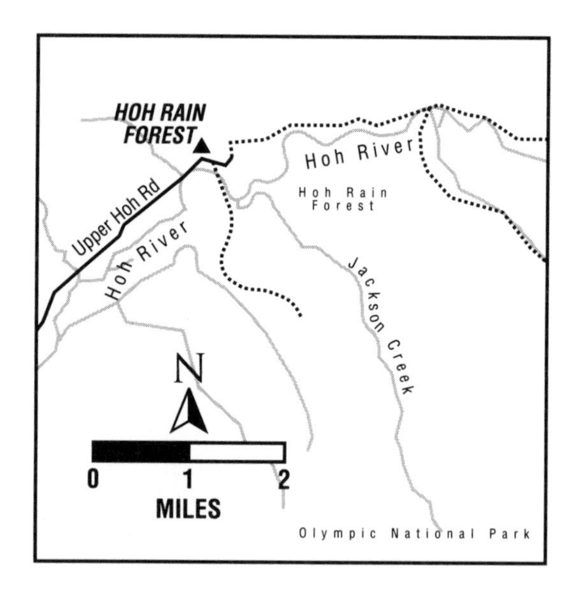

The Hoh Rain Forest Visitor Center and Campground will probably be one of the busiest facilities you'll come across in this book. The rain forest attracts visitors from all over the world, but its uniqueness warrants inclusion in this car camping guide. Summer is the season of highest volume, naturally, but the visitor center and campground are open year-round, so you may want to plan a visit in the off-season.

Temperatures are never really hot or cold at any time of the year in the Hoh Valley, but spending time here in seasons other than summer and late spring means limiting your hiking options to low elevations. The Hoh River Valley itself is a grand off-season walk, with roundtrip distances up to 18 miles without significant altitude gain. In the immediate vicinity of the visitor center are three short nature trails of varying lengths that render fine examples of rain forest vegetation. Elk can often be observed on these short trips.

For the more energetic backpackers who come to the Hoh in the summer, Hoh River Trail has become the most popular access to Mount Olympus (mainly because it is the shortest way in from a road-end). It's 18.5 miles one way to Blue Glacier at the base of the east peak of Mount Olympus. The Hoh trail also connects with other major (trunk) trails in the park. Backcountry permits are required for any overnight travel on trails. Check with a park ranger for further information if you plan extended backpack trips within the park. The nearest spot for supplies is Westward Hoh (5.6 miles from the intersection with U.S. 101).

You are advised not to attempt boating or swimming in the Hoh River because it moves rapidly and is very cold and often jammed with logs. Fishing is, however, one safe option, and a list of regulations is available at the visitor center.

It's several hours by car from metropolitan Puget Sound to the Hoh River Road turnoff. Unless you already plan to be on the peninsula, this is easily a weekend outing.

To get there from either north or south, take U.S. 101 around Olympic Peninsula to the west side of Olympic National Park. Turn east onto Upper Hoh Road about 18 miles south of the town of Forks; the campground is at the end of the road. Driving distance from Seattle by way of Olympia is roughly 200 miles; by way of Washington State ferries to Winslow or Kingston, the road distance is about 145 miles. Ferry crossings take about a half-hour.

KEY INFORMATION

Hoh Rain Forest Campground
Hoh Visitor Center
c/o Olympic National Park
Port Angeles, WA 98362

Operated by: Hoh Ranger Station, Olympic National Park, National Park Service, U.S. Department of Interior

Information: (360) 374-6925, ranger station; (360) 452-4501, park headquarters

Open: All year

Individual sites: 89

Each site has: Fire grill, picnic table

Site assignment: First come, first served; no reservations

Registration: Self-registration at bulletin board next to restrooms

Facilities: Restrooms with flush toilets, sinks, disabled access; RV dump station; summer naturalist program; visitor center

Parking: At individual sites

Fee: $10 per night

Elevation: 578 feet

Restrictions:

Pets–On leash at all times; not allowed on trails or in public buildings

Fires–In fire pits

Alcoholic beverages–Permitted

Vehicles–RVs up to 21 feet; no hookups

Other–Do not feed birds or animals; permits required for overnight hikes

ILLAHEE STATE PARK

Bremerton, Washington

Here is one of those classic spots of the Northwest that makes car camping on a moment's notice in this region such a delightful proposition.

Situated on a high bluff that guards the southern entrance to Port Orchard Bay, Illahee State Park is a gem of a destination roughly an hour by ferry west of Seattle and about half that amount of time if you're driving north from Tacoma. Or you can get there by ferry on the Edmonds/Kingston run (just north of Seattle) and sightsee your way south through an interesting collection of side trips. With 1,785 feet of saltwater frontage on the bay and a 354-foot dock accompanied by a flotilla of moorage buoys, you could even slip into this quiet haven by boat.

The park faces northeast, tucked out of the way on the northern outskirts of Bremerton and overlooking the backside of Bainbridge Island. Until recently, Bremerton was known mostly to the outside world as a ship-building port and home to the Navy's Pacific fleet. But a national magazine recently included Bremerton in its top ten most livable cities in America. There went the neighborhood!

However, the throngs have yet to descend on Illahee (a Native American term for "earth" or "country"), and it still appears to be unknown to

CAMPGROUND RATINGS

Beauty:	★★★★★
Site privacy:	★★★★
Site spaciousness:	★★★★
Quiet:	★★★★
Security:	★★★★
Cleanliness/upkeep:	★★★★★
Insect control:	★★★

Undiscovered yet convenient, this lovely place is for those who don't feel they have to drive endless hours to get away from it all.

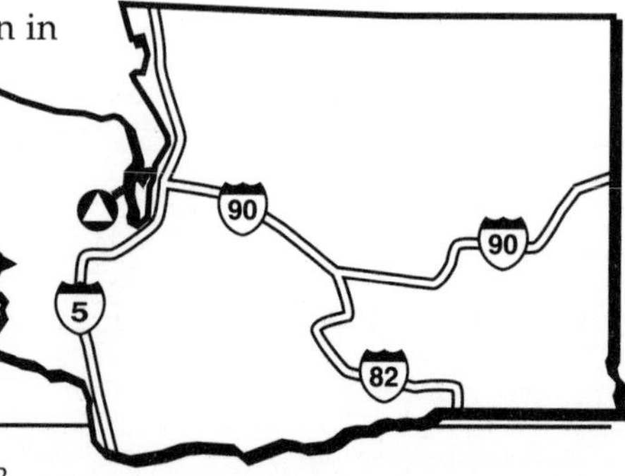

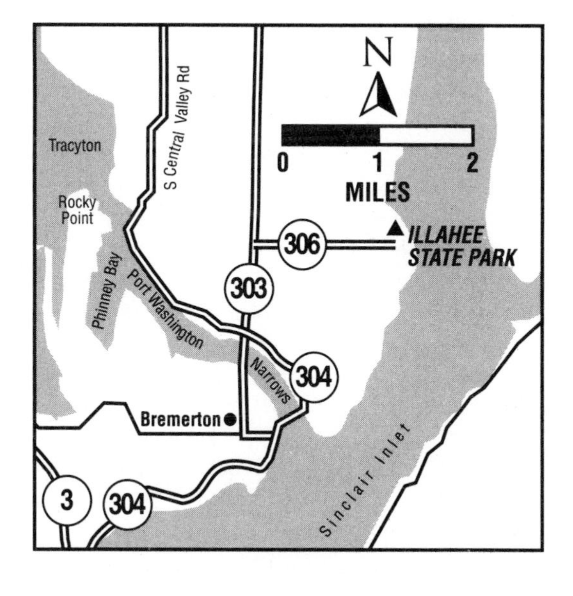

most out-of-towners. On a gorgeous weekday in late summer, there were a handful of kids in day camp–type groups, a few fishermen on the pier, and a number of empty campsites.

For those who don't feel that they need to drive endless hours to get away, Illahee is the perfect retreat amidst towering and densely clustered maples, cedars, Douglas fir, madrona, dogwood, and rhododendron. Ferns, salal, huckleberry, blackberry, and salmonberry provide heavy doses of understory for each of the picturesque and very private campsites.

William Bremer, for whom Bremerton is named, first settled in the area around 1888 and salivated at the abundant timber resources. Fortunately he set to work clearing other areas first, and Illahee was spared the ax and chainsaw. The state acquired the park in seven separate parcels, beginning in 1934; much of the original foliage was left intact.

After setting up camp and with the sound of seagulls screeching overhead, take one of the park trails that leads down to the waterfront. The drop is steep, so you'll get that much-needed exercise. There is a paved roadway down to the water as well, but I advise using the path if you intend to walk. The road is sharply inclined and narrow with no accommodation for pedestrians. It could be a bit daunting to meet up with a truck-and-boat trailer combination on any of the several blind, hairpin turns along the way.

Park developers got a little carried away with the size of the parking lot down at the beach, but in all likelihood this was done to accommodate the number of boaters using the launch area on busy summer weekends. It's a prime spot to put in and explore the shorelines along the numerous bays, inlets, and passages of Puget Sound. Sea kayaking is an excellent consideration from this spot, too.

There's plenty of marine life and the usual assortment of parklike creatures on shore (squirrels, chipmunks, and raccoons) to observe. At low tide, the clamming can be quite good. Crabbing and oystering are options, but check with park officials before eating any shellfish. A condition known as "red tide" and occasional pollution plague beaches around Puget Sound on an indiscriminate basis. Generally there will be signs posted warning of any current hazards.

Points of interest in the surrounding areas include quaint Scandinavian Poulsbo, the town of Suquamish, antiques malls in Port Orchard, Trident Submarine Warfare Base in Bangor, and the Thomas Kemper Brewing Company (one of the first microbreweries established in the Seattle area). A number of first-class golf courses are within a short drive of the campground.

To get there from the ferry terminal, follow SR 303 north (Warren Avenue) to SR 306 (Sylvan Way). Turn right, and follow the signs to Illahee. Total distance from the ferry terminal is about 3 miles.

To get there from Tacoma, cross the Tacoma Narrows Bridge on SR 16 and follow it for about 25 miles to Bremerton. Take the "City Center" exit (SR 304), which zigzags confusingly through town. Just keep making the obvious zigzags until you reach SR 303 (Warren Avenue). Turn left, and follow the directions above.

KEY INFORMATION

Illahee State Park
3540 Bahia Vista
Bremerton, WA 98310

Operated by: Washington State Parks and Recreation Commission

Information: (360) 902-8500 or (360) 478-6460

Open: All year

Individual sites: 25 standard, 8 primitive

Each site has: Fire grill, picnic table, water, shade trees

Site assignment: First come, first served; no reservations

Registration: Self-registration on site

Facilities: Restrooms with toilets, sinks, hot showers; boat launch, mooring buoys, boat dock; public telephone; trailer dump station; horseshoe pits, ball field, playground; group picnic areas with covered kitchens; disabled access

Parking: At individual sites and in parking lot at shoreline

Fee: $10 standard, $15 hookup; $5 each additional vehicle; $5 primitive, $7 drive-up primitive

Elevation: 500 feet

Restrictions:

Pets–On leash

Fires–In fire pit

Alcoholic beverages–Only in designated areas

Vehicles–RVs up to 30 feet

LARRABEE STATE PARK

Bellingham, Washington

Camping within 7 miles of an urban center may not exactly be your idea of a wilderness escape. But when time, inclination, or myriad other factors don't allow you to throw yourself into a far-flung adventure, the unspoiled pleasure of Larrabee State Park can be quite a respectable substitute.

Located on 1,885 acres along the saltwater shores of Samish Bay south of Bellingham, Larrabee is the oldest state park in Washington. Its designation in 1915 has kept protected throughout the years such a lush growth of Northwest foliage—Douglas fir, western red cedar, alder, hemlock, bigleaf maple, willows, rhododendron, and sword fern—that it is difficult not to think that you have ventured miles into a remote and primeval place.

In reality, the way to Larrabee is along one of the most heavily traveled scenic drives in western Washington and perhaps in the entire state. Chuckanut Drive, also known as State Route 11, connects south Bellingham with the tiny farming communities of the Skagit River flats in 25 miles of roadway that cling precariously to the side of Chuckanut Mountain. A series of wheel-gripping twists and turns eventually gives way to a straightaway that makes you accelerate just for the sheer joy of seeing broad, flat ground all around you.

CAMPGROUND RATINGS

Beauty:	★★★★★
Site privacy:	★★★★
Site spaciousness:	★★★★
Quiet:	★★★
Security:	★★★
Cleanliness/upkeep:	★★★★★
Insect control:	★★★

Only seven miles from Bellingham, this park will give you a respectable nature fix when you're on a tight schedule.

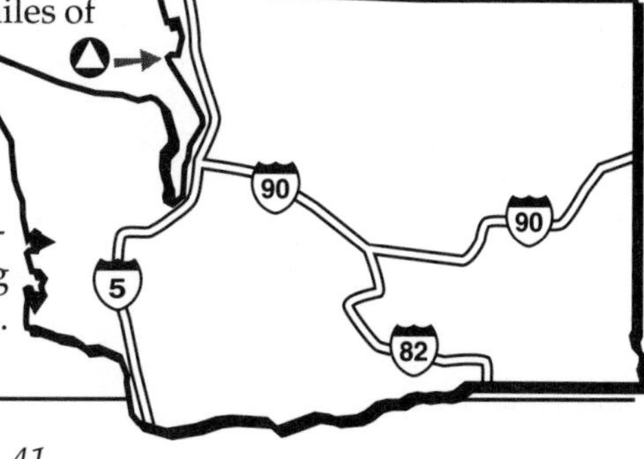

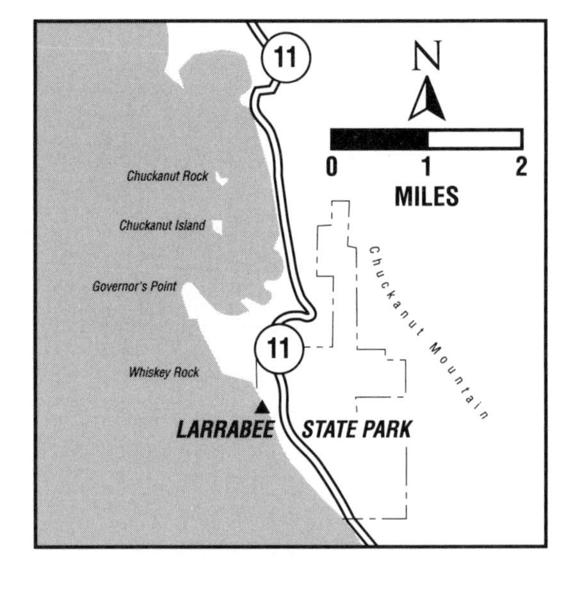

Chuckanut Drive is famous not only for its suicide turns but also for the stupendous views across Puget Sound to the San Juan archipelago. A couple of first-rate seafood restaurants along Chuckanut also make the drive a popular outing, but they are easy to miss if you're looking for them for the first time. You may be too busy watching the brake lights of the car in front of you as you crawl along with the rest of the weekend cruisers.

For reasons that defy explanation, this stretch of roadway attracts a sizable number of cyclists. I don't recommend it myself simply because it is too dangerous. The road is very narrow with minimal shoulders, blind corners, and too many lurching RVs for my tastes. Aside from an occasional turnout, there is no place to go to avoid or be avoided short of slamming into the crumbling rock of Chuckanut Mountain or over a guardrail into space. A "Bike Route" marker does not a bike route make, in my opinion.

So leave the bicycle at home on this trip. You have plenty of hiking trails, pebbled beaches, and rocky tide pools to explore instead. Sea kayaking is also an option with numerous coves, bays, points, rocks, and islets within easy paddling range. For the fishermen and women, there's the saltwater version of a boat launch nearby. For freshwater anglers, both Fragrance Lake and Lost Lake are stocked, but you have to take a 2-mile trail to reach them. Birdwatching, swimming, and scuba diving have their seasonal appeal.

If you simply want fresh air and a look at the lay of the land, take a drive up Cleator Road to 1,900-foot Cyrus Gates Overlook for the best possible view of the San Juans. For views of Mount Baker (Washington's third highest volcanic peak, only 30 air miles east) and the North Cascade Range, take the short trail to the East Overlook.

Weatherwise, this is coastal western Washington, so let's be realistic. Westerly winds carry moisture and cool temperatures most of the year, with late summer and early fall the most dependable times for dry tenting. Even on the hottest summer days, marine breezes chill the skin, and it is a rare evening that doesn't warrant a sweater or jacket. Evening lasts a long time in the summer. It is not uncommon to be able to see the last streaks of a fabulous sunset as late as 11 p.m.

While reservations are not usually necessary at Larrabee State Park, you are advised that summer months are the busiest.

Note: At press time, the campground was undergoing renovations that were expected to be completed by mid- to late 1996.

To get there, drive north on I-5 to the turnoff for Chuckanut Drive and Fairhaven. Follow the signs to SR 11, and head south. The entrance to the park is about 7 miles on the right.

KEY INFORMATION

Larrabee State Park
245 Chuckanut Drive
Bellingham, WA 98225

Operated by: Washington State Parks and Recreation Commission

Information: (360) 676-2093

Open: All year

Individual sites: 74; 26 are separate RV sites with hookups

Each site has: Picnic table, fire pit with grill, shade trees

Site assignment: First come, first served; reservations accepted, call (800) 452-5687, $6 fee

Registration: Self-registration on site

Facilities: Bathhouse with sinks, toilets, showers, hot water; firewood; boat launch nearby

Parking: At individual site

Fee: $11 per night; $15 full hook-up

Elevation: Sea level

Restrictions:

Pets–On leash

Fires–In fire pits only

Alcoholic beverages–Permitted

Vehicles–No limit on RV size

LOWER LEWIS RIVER FALLS RECREATION AREA

Swift, Washington

Not long after the eruption of Mount St. Helens, a small plane carried its umpteenth load of international news reporters and photographers on a media junket into the area of devastation. A local reporter familiar with the Northwest terrain was among the group. As the plane flew over vast tracts of gouged landscapes and treeless mountainsides, all except the local reporter gasped and swore softly at the destruction they witnessed below them. They took copious notes and jammed camera lenses up against the plane's windows, firing off numerous rounds of film with their motor drives.

Only the local reporter sat calmly and, at one point, quietly informed the rest of his comrades that they were a long way from the Mount St. Helens zone. What they saw below, he explained, were rather typical examples of a Northwest clearcut.

They may very well have been flying up the Lewis River valley.

Now that I've been up there myself, I really think the best time to head for the Lower Lewis River Falls Recreation Area is about midnight on a moonless night. All along SR 503 (Lewis River Road), which sidehills along huge reservoirs and looks across to what is left of this section of Gifford Pinchot National Forest, it is evident that any idea of discussing the spotted owl as an endangered species over coffee in

CAMPGROUND RATINGS

Beauty:	★★★★★
Site privacy:	★★★★
Site spaciousness:	★★★★★
Quiet:	★★★★★
Security:	★★★
Cleanliness/upkeep:	★★★★★
Insect control:	★★★★

A good site for a base camp while you explore Mount St. Helens, this area also offers major waterfall viewing and lots of other outdoor activities.

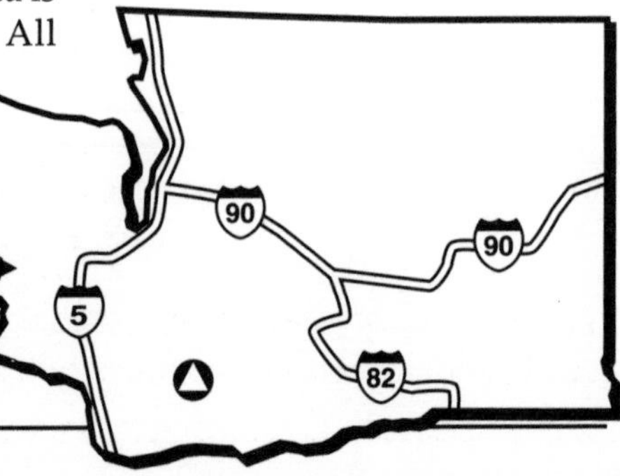

the Cougar cafe is a foolish notion. Logging is king around here—at least while this book is current.

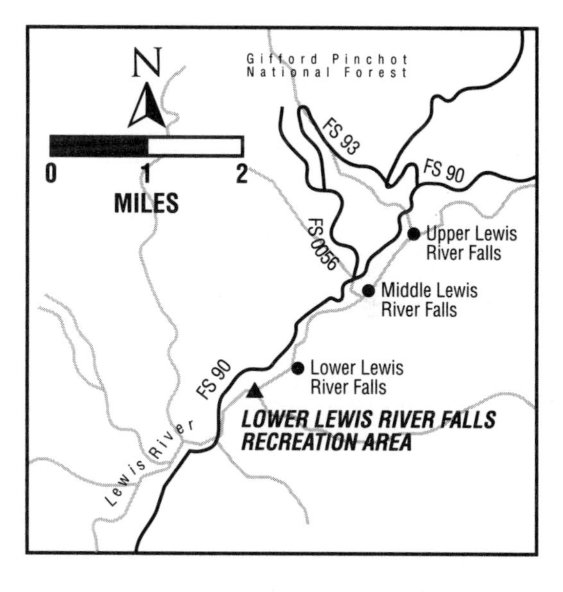

Unfortunately on cloudy days (which are frequent in this mountainous western Washington terrain), there isn't much to look at on the way to the Lower Falls area except the expansive reservoirs and the clearcut hills. However, if you are blessed with fewer clouds on your trip, views of Mount St. Helens appear at various points along the route. Some of them are even marked. Take every opportunity you have to stop and enjoy the vista. Once at the falls, you'll be deep in the woods where views of mountain peaks are quickly diminished.

There the primary spectacle becomes a series of major waterfalls roaring off what are known geologically as "benches," wide tiers of rock formed over many thousands of years as glaciers and the Lewis River carved out the steep-sided V-shaped valley. The Forest Service has an extensive list of the waterfalls in the area, many of which are within an easy walk of Forest Service roads.

I have been to the lower of the three Lewis River Falls only at low-water times of the year—summer, to be exact. Much of the rock is exposed during low-runoff periods, but this makes for equally interesting viewing. The rock is worn smooth and polished, appearing as a huge mass of flat-topped pillows. It is easy to imagine the thunderous splendor of these falls when water levels are high. Late spring would be the best time to see them in their glory.

Lower Lewis River Falls Recreation Area has undergone some renovation recently and sports twice as many campsites as before. The original 20 are still the best because they are closer to the river and have more vegetation between them for ultimate privacy. Once the new sites get some undergrowth between them, they'll be adequate. For now, let the RVs have them.

Keep in mind that this is a campground with few amenities and one step up from the primitive category. Supplies are a long way back at Cougar (and they are limited even there), so plan to go in well-prepared.

Activities in the Lewis River valley—aside from waterfall viewing—include hiking, fishing, hunting, horsepacking, canoeing, and volcano watching. There are endless trails in the neighborhood, some of which pass through the campground. The Lewis River Trail is a popular, low-elevation meander for 9 miles. The river offers good trout and salmon catches at designated spots.

The Upper Lewis River canoe route can be a challenging 8 miles when heavy snowmelt turns some Class II stretches into Class IV. Check out the Mount St. Helens National Volcanic Monument Center in Swift if you are using the Recreation Area as a base camp to visit this modern-day geologic phenomenon. Give yourself several days just for Mount St. Helens. If you're interested in climbing the mountain, stop in at Jack's Restaurant on SR 503 west of Cougar for all the information (and permits) you'll need.

To get there, take the Woodland exit off I-5, and follow SR 503 (Lewis River Road) to Cougar—about 45 miles. SR 503 beyond Cougar becomes FS 90. The campground is another 28 miles past Cougar on the Forest Service Road.

KEY INFORMATION

Lower Lewis River Falls Recreation Area
c/o Mount St. Helens National Volcanic Monument
42218 N.E. Yale Bridge Road
Amboy, WA 98601

Operated by: Mount St. Helens National Volcanic Monument

Information: (360) 750-3900

Open: Memorial Day through October

Individual sites: 43

Each site has: Fire pit, picnic table

Site assignment: First come, first served; reservations accepted

Registration: Self-registration on site

Facilities: Piped water, pit toilets, firewood, disabled access

Parking: At individual sites

Fee: $9

Elevation: 1,450

Restrictions:

Pets–On leash

Fires–In fire pits

Alcoholic beverages–Permitted

Vehicles–RVs up to 20 feet

Other–Permits required for climbing Mount St. Helens

MERRILL LAKE CAMPGROUND

Cougar, Washington

In May 1980, Mount St. Helens forever altered the landscape for miles around when it erupted in the worst natural disaster that western Washington is likely to see for a very long time. Only one other time in the recorded history of volcanic activity has a mountain exploded the way St. Helens did—more out of its side than its top. The blast (500 times greater than the force of the atomic bomb on Hiroshima) spewed billions of tons of debris northward and created a fan-shaped path of destruction that stretched over 150 square miles from northwest to northeast.

In the aftermath, St. Helens looked as if it had been savagely disemboweled with a giant scoop. Between the jagged south rim—lowered to 8,400 feet—and what was left of anything remotely mountain-like on the north rim at 6,800 feet were the remnants of the previous 9,677-foot peak. The view from the north showed a gaping amphitheater-like hollow, blackened beyond belief and measuring 1 mile wide by 2 miles long. Only seconds before, this had been a scene of tranquil, snow-capped symmetry.

Had Mount St. Helens chosen to send its pyroclastic plume in any other direction, it is highly doubtful that areas to the south (including the subject of this listing) would have been as remarkably untouched as they were. Aside from mudflows

CAMPGROUND RATINGS

Beauty:	★★★★
Site privacy:	★★★★
Site spaciousness:	★★★★★
Quiet:	★★★★★
Security:	★★
Cleanliness/upkeep:	★★★★
Insect control:	★★★

Primitive and remote, this campground south of Mount St. Helens lets you explore the area in relative tourist-free solitude.

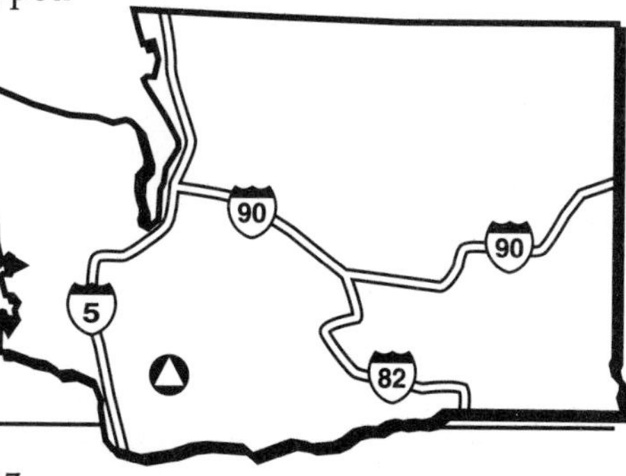

and flooding down the Kalama River, Lewis River, and Swift Creek watershed, these sections of federal- and state-managed lands sustained surprisingly little long-term damage.

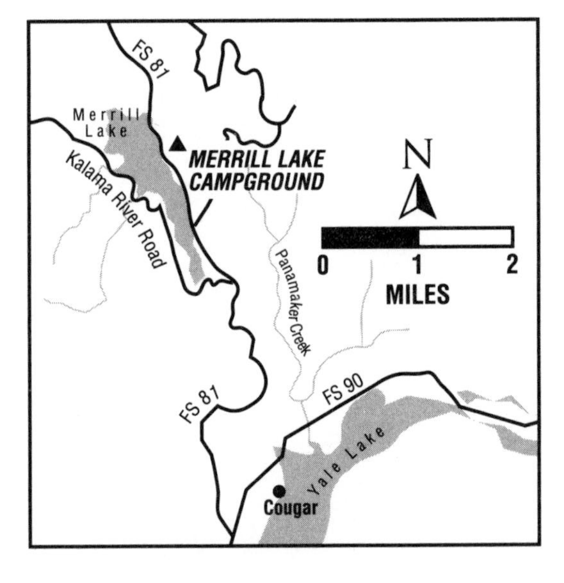

In fact, campers who were enjoying the serene quiet of Merrill Lake on that fateful May morning must have been doing so with one eye nervously fixed in the direction of the mountain (which is roughly 6 air miles to the northeast). A "red zone" had recently been established within 5 miles of the steaming crater, and only scientists and law enforcement officials were allowed inside it. When the mountain blew, those lucky enough to have chosen a weekend outing on the south side probably thought that the plume of ash rising to an eventual height of 63,000 feet was the extent of the show. It wouldn't be until they returned home later that evening that television news reports showed them the full extent of the horror.

Today, more than a decade later, Merrill Lake Campground sits in wooded isolation just outside the boundaries of Gifford Pinchot National Forest and Mount St. Helens National Volcanic Monument. Recreational options around Merrill Lake include hiking on high- and lowland trails, boating, fishing, mountain biking, cross-country skiing, and caving. Since the campground is open all year, doesn't require reservations, doesn't charge a fee, and is located just above sea level in the Cascade foothills, it can be a good off-season choice.

In summer, most of the tourist throngs inundate Mount St. Helens from the north, leaving you to explore lands around the geologic wonder in relative solitude. Short drives up Forest Service roads lead to such interesting natural features as Ape Cave, a 2-mile lava tube that is representative of past volcanic activity. On the same road to Ape Cave is the Trail of Two Forests, a self-interpretive walk over a 2,000-year-old lava bed. A short way up FS 24, which heads north from Lewis River Road at the east end of Swift Creek Reservoir, is the trailhead to Cedar Flats. This is a looped stroll through old-growth Douglas fir in Cedar Flats Northern Research Natural Area. These are wintering grounds for Roosevelt elk.

If you're into some serious driving and want the best views of the Mount St. Helens devastation, take FS 25 north to its intersection with FS 99. This route takes you deep into the area of destruction to a viewpoint at Windy Ridge. These Forest Service roads are gravel, and sections are closed in winter. For full information on traveling either by foot or car in Mount St. Helens National Volcanic Monument, it is best to contact the park directly for current conditions. There is a park visitor center in Swift.

To get there, take Lewis River Road east from Woodland off I-5 to the small settlement of Cougar. Turn north, away from Yale Lake, onto FR 81, and travel 4.5 miles to the access road that leads to the campground.

KEY INFORMATION

Merrill Lake Campground
c/o Department of Natural Resources
AW-11, 1065 South Capitol Way
Olympia, WA 98504

Operated by: Department of Natural Resources

Information: (800) 527-3305 in Washington; (360) 577-2025

Open: April to October, depending on weather

Individual sites: 11

Each site has: Picnic table, fire grill, tent pads

Site assignment: First come, first served; no reservations

Registration: Not necessary

Facilities: Piped water, firewood, pit toilets, boat launch, disabled access

Parking: At individual sites

Fee: No fee

Elevation: 1,650 feet

Restrictions:

Pets–On leash

Fires–In fire pits only

Alcoholic beverages–Permitted

Vehicles–Small RVs recommended

MORA CAMPGROUND

La Push, Washington

CAMPGROUND RATINGS

Beauty:	★★★★★
Site privacy:	★★★★
Site spaciousness:	★★★★
Quiet:	★★★★★
Security:	★★★
Cleanliness/upkeep:	★★★★
Insect control:	★★★★★

No other public campground in Washington State brings you in such close driving proximity to wilderness beaches that are accessible only by foot both north and south.

Grab your Gore-Tex for this one! We're heading for the wet and wild (or, should I say, wetter and wilder?) side of Olympic National Park to some of the last stretches of coastal wilderness left in the contiguous United States.

Mora Campground, part of the network of well-attended Olympic National Park facilities, is among the elite when it comes to its location only a mile or so from the Pacific Ocean. For a total of 57 unspoiled and challenging miles (from the Quillayute River north to the boundary of the Makah Indian Reservation and south to the legendary Hoh River and its namesake tribal grounds), the saltwater frontage of the Pacific Ocean is a panoply of protruding headlands, swirling tidepools, crashing surf, and stalwart "seastacks."

For many years, this outpost from civilization was an active trading port up the Quillayute River for ships from Seattle. When neither roads nor rail materialized, access other than by boat kept Mora secluded from further development.

In recent history (1990), a pall was cast over certain sections of the coastal parklands when a major oil spill occurred near Cape Flattery (the northwesternmost piece of land in the lower 48 states). It will never be the same, but the latest reports seem to indicate that much of

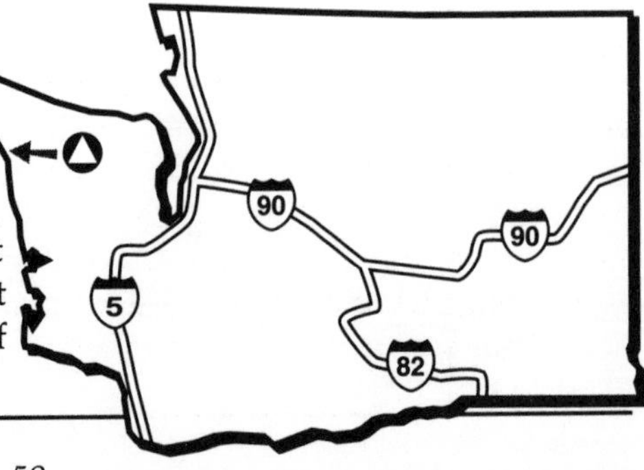

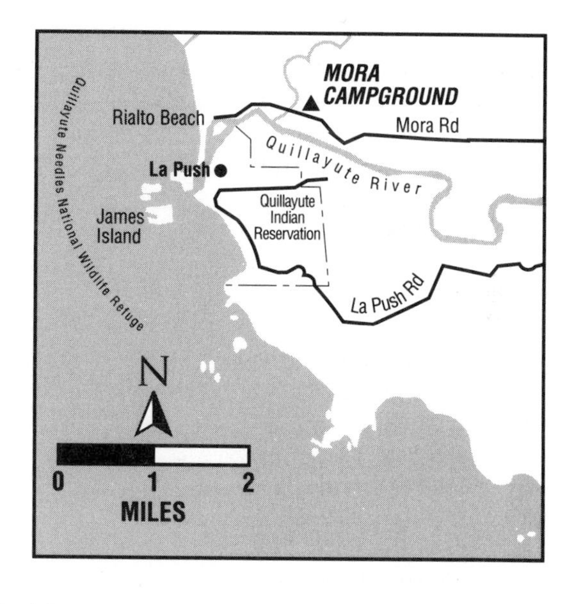

the oil was controlled and scooped up, thanks to the quick response of various agencies.

Fortunately this is still one of the truly remarkable and entrancing spots in the country, perhaps even in the world. The blend of natural geography, cultural influence, and historical record are a powerful combination.

The weather-beaten Washington coast can be a formidable presence even in its most timid mood. This is a place where rain slickers, wool sweaters, waterproof footwear, and a hat you can hold onto are very much in order any time of the year. Western winds hit the coast unchecked and work the surf into a foaming frenzy. As a result, the shape of the coastline is forever changing.

Mora Campground is a relatively large complex compared with other Olympic Park accommodations. Situated at sea level, Mora is open all year and is an ideal choice for off-season travel. Actually, winter months and early spring can be some of the best times weatherwise at the Washington coast. You'll have an opportunity to watch the migratory gray whales that pass on their way to southern California and Mexico.

A word of warning: Coastal hiking requires a tide table at all times of the year. Many of the points, bluffs, heads, and capes are covered at high tide, and you'll need to either wait out the tide or, where possible, go overland to continue. Even the inland routes can be muddy and treacherous, so make sure you have good traction on your shoes or boots. The "Strip of Wilderness" brochure available at the Mora Ranger Station is full of information about the pleasures and precautions of coastal hiking.

Check at either the Mora station or information stations along U.S. 101—there's one north of Forks and one at Kalaloch—for other options in this part of Olympic National Park and the surrounding National Forest.

One last word: The Indian reservations that border the Park along the coast are private property.

To get there from either north or south, take U.S. 101 around the Olympic Peninsula to the town of Forks (between 125 and 200 miles from Seattle, depending on which route you take). About 1 mile north of Forks, turn west onto La Push Road, and drive for about 10 miles to Mora Road. Turn right onto Mora Road, and follow the signs to the campground.

KEY INFORMATION

Mora Campground
c/o Mora Ranger Station
3283 Mora Road
Forks, WA 98331

Operated by: Olympic National Park, National Park Service, U.S. Department of the Interior

Information: (360) 374-5460

Open: All year

Individual sites: 94

Each site has: Fire grill, picnic table

Site assignment: First come, first served; no reservations

Registration: Self-registration on site

Facilities: Bathhouse with toilets, sinks, running water, drinking water, disabled access; group camp

Parking: At individual sites

Fee: $10 per night

Elevation: Sea level

Restrictions:

Pets–On leash

Fires–In fire pits

Alcoholic beverages–Permitted

Vehicles–RVs up to 21 feet; no vehicles allowed off park roads

Other–Permits required for extended hikes

PANORAMA POINT CAMPGROUND

Baker Lake, Washington

Many purist Northwest wilderness goers purposefully overlook camping options at places like Baker Lake simply because they don't feel that they're truly getting a pristine experience if they're within earshot of mechanized sounds.

In the case of Panorama Point Campground midway up the western shore, that sound will most likely be the gentle buzz of small outboard motors as fishermen putt-putt around in search of the best spots to hook their daily catch. They have their choice of such delights as rainbow, cutthroat, or Dolly Varden trout; kokanee salmon; and whitefish.

This is, indeed, a fisherman's lake. But with miles and miles of Forest Service roads and trails that take you to soothing hot springs and deep into two designated wildernesses, a national recreation area, a national park, and along the lake's undeveloped eastern shore, one can hardly complain that there's just no getting away from things here. Just make sure you have a good Forest Service map and trail guides of the area before you find yourself at the mercy of the purists.

To the west of Panorama Point lies the glacier-encrusted mass of Mount Baker. This is Washington State's third highest volcano and active only thermally as far as geolo-

CAMPGROUND RATINGS

Beauty:	★★★★★
Site privacy:	★★★★
Site spaciousness:	★★★★
Quiet:	★★★
Security:	★★★★
Cleanliness/upkeep:	★★★★★
Insect control:	★★★

This is a fisherman's lake, but there's lots for others to do, too.

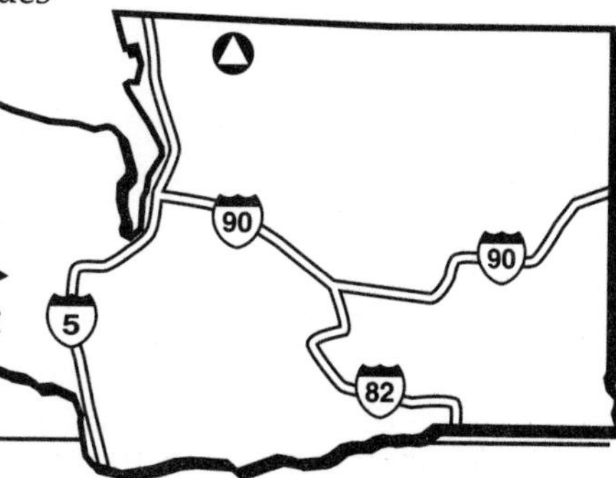

gists can determine. Designated wilderness surrounds Mount Baker and is adjacent to national recreation areas on both north and south flanks of the mountain. Here you'll find unlimited hiking, backpacking, skiing, and climbing opportunities, depending on which season you choose to travel.

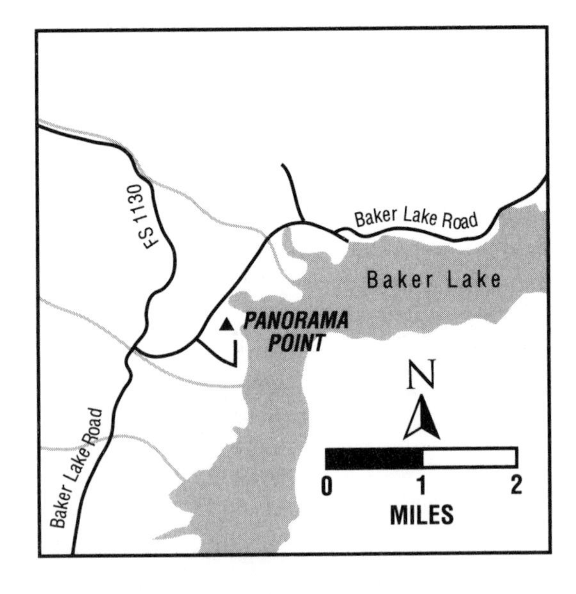

It's best to check with appropriate agencies that jurisdict these areas for special conditions and restrictions that may prevail. Backpackers, for instance, will need permits for overnight trips into the backcountry.

North of the campground is equally spectacular Mount Shuksan, a craggy sentinel of snow, ice, and rock that is the gateway for foot travelers approaching North Cascades National Park from the west. There could be no more fitting prototype to the challenging terrain than that embodied in names like Mount Despair, Damnation Park, Mount Challenger, Mount Terror, Mount Fury, and Jagged Ridge. These are but a few of the numerous natural shrines in the northern sector of North Cascades National Park that have been immortalized in the minds and journals of many a mountaineer.

East across Baker Lake is the smallest of the eight wilderness areas in the Mount Baker-Snoqualmie National Forest. Despite its diminutive size (14,300 acres), the Noisy-Diobsud Wilderness is a place to be reckoned with. Elevations range from 2,000 to 6,234 feet, with only 2 miles of maintained trails. It is, for all intents and purposes, a place for experienced climbers and scramblers who are looking for their own versions of steep and deep.

The entire expanse of national forest and parklands around Panorama Point can be quite wet and chilly. Although the campground is only 800 feet in elevation, conditions are more representative of those higher up because the lake captures moisture-laden clouds that drift into the lake basin. Rainfall averages 40 inches in the lowlands, with up to 100 inches of snow recorded regularly at the highest points.

Lush vegetation is the result of all this moisture, but much of the land remains heavily forested due to the extreme contours that make logging an expensive operation.

To get there, drive north on Baker Lake Road from its junction with SR 20 about 6 miles west of Concrete (named for the primary industry that converts local limestone into cement).

KEY INFORMATION

Panorama Point Campground
c/o Mount Baker Ranger District
2105 Highway 20
Sedro Woolley, WA 98284

Operated by: Mount Baker-Snoqualmie National Forest; Conservation Resources, Inc. provides concession service in summer

Information: (360) 856-5700

Open: May to October

Individual sites: 16

Each site has: Picnic table, fire pit with grill, shade trees

Site assignment: First come, first served; reservations accepted, call (800) 280-CAMP

Registration: Self-registration on site

Facilities: Flush toilets, piped water; firewood; store, cafe, and ice within 1 mile; boat dock nearby

Parking: At individual sites

Fee: $10 per night

Elevation: 800 feet

Restrictions:

Pets–On leash

Fires–In fire pit only

Alcoholic beverages–Permitted

Vehicles–RVs and trailers up to 21 feet

Other–Permits required for overnight backpacking

SPENCER SPIT STATE PARK

Lopez, Washington

A book about car camping in the Northwest would not be complete without at least one listing from the beautiful San Juan Islands archipelago. The selection of one is relatively easy, actually, despite the fact that the San Juan Islands have an official count of 768 exposed rocks, reefs, and islands that make up the chain.

For starters, only 175 of these land formations have been named, and 85 are inaccessible to the public with protection under a designation as the San Juan Islands National Wildlife Refuge. Only four can be reached by commercial ferry either from Anacortes, Washington, on the U.S. side or Sidney, British Columbia, on the Canadian side. Of these four, only three maintained campgrounds are accessible by car. The rest are boat-in only.

That leaves Spencer Spit State Park on Lopez Island.

Far from the seasonal rat race and the city-like atmosphere of the much larger but filled-to-overflowing facilities on Orcas and San Juan Islands, Spencer Spit is an excellent base camp for enjoying Lopez and its sister islands by car, foot, or bicycle.

The only drawback to lovely little Spencer Spit is the same drawback that plagues all of the other islands that are served by the same method—the Washington State ferry system.

CAMPGROUND RATINGS

Beauty:	★★★★★
Site privacy:	★★★★
Site spaciousness:	★★★★
Quiet:	★★★★★
Security:	★★★
Cleanliness/upkeep:	★★★★
Insect control:	★★★★

If you want to see the beautiful San Juan Islands archipelago, this is the place to stay. You can camp right on the beach.

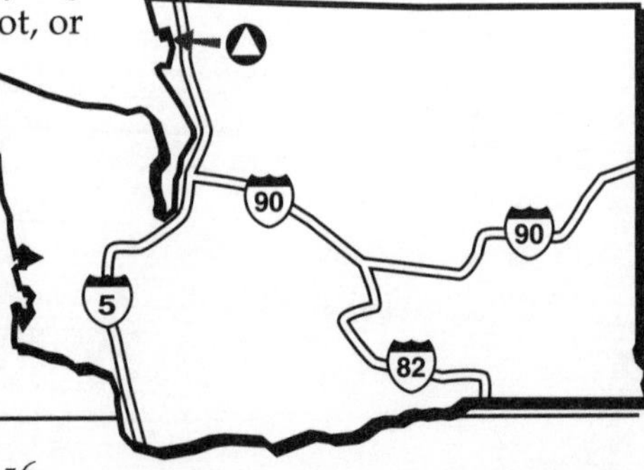

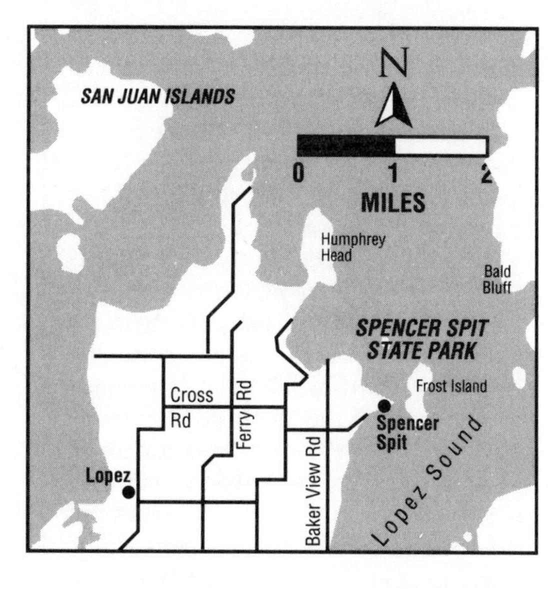

First, plan on becoming a veritable scholar of the ferry schedule. Pick one up when you pay at the tollbooth. Make sure you know that where you want to go is also where the ferry is planning to go. Ditto on when. In the summertime, additional ferries are put on high-volume routes to accommodate the heavy onslaught of tourists and vacationers. This does not mean that all ferries stop at all islands all the time, however. Some ferries stop at some of the islands some of the time. Lopez is one of those "some of the time" islands.

One of the most appealing aspects of Spencer Spit State Park is that you can camp right on the beach—in designated areas, of course. You will have to pack your gear down from the parking lot above.

Lopez Island is, in my estimation, the premier bicycling island of the San Juans and can easily be covered in a day of riding if you're accustomed to 40 miles or so. Except for the hill up from the ferry terminal, which you will most likely ascend by car anyway, Lopez is mildly rolling hills of farmland with paved roads and a noticeable lack of traffic—even on weekends. It's possible that you'll encounter more bicycles than cars on any given day during the summer.

One of my favorite pastimes on Lopez is to ride out to Shark Reef Park with the "3 Bs"—a book, a pair of binoculars, and a brown-bag lunch—to watch the sea lions that sprawl *en masse* on the offshore rocks. From your vantage point at Shark Reef, you can also look far across the San Juan Channel to windswept Cattle Point on San Juan Island, where the only sand dunes in the entire island group exist.

Other points of interest on Lopez Island include the village of Lopez with some excellent restaurants, interesting shops, and a small museum. Richardson and Mackaye Harbor at the island's southern tip are also highly scenic spots easily reached by car or bicycle. The ferry from Lopez takes you directly into Friday Harbor on San Juan Island and Orcas on (what else?) Orcas Island, both thriving business districts. Unless you're interested in touring the other islands extensively, it's fastest and cheapest just to walk onto the ferry from Lopez and kick around Friday Harbor and Orcas on foot.

The climate of the San Juan Islands is practically in a class by itself. Although westerly marine winds can bring a change in the weather at any time, the islands are part of the dry "rain shadow" effect from the Olympic Mountains that extends northeast across the Strait of Juan de Fuca. As a result, rainfall averages only about 15 to 25 inches per year. Summers can be quite hot—some of my deepest tans are from San Juan bicycle trips—and the lovely, balmy days of autumn are unsurpassed. Even in summer, however, nights are chilly enough for a campfire to be appreciated.

To get there from the ferry terminal at the north end of Lopez Island, take Ferry Road south, and follow the signs to the park. The total distance from ferry terminal is barely 5 miles.

KEY INFORMATION

Spencer Spit State Park
Route 2, Box 3600
Lopez, WA 98261

Operated by: Washington State Parks and Recreation Commission

Information: (360) 468-2251

Open: March to October

Individual sites: 41

Each site has: Fire grill, picnic table

Site assignment: Reservations, call (800) 452-5687, $6 fee

Registration: Self-registration on site

Facilities: Bathhouse with sinks, toilets

Parking: In campground and at some individual sites; parking for beach sites near trailhead

Fee: $8 per night

Elevation: Sea level

Restrictions:

Pets–On leash

Fires–In fire pits

Alcoholic beverages–Permitted

Vehicles–Self-contained RVs up to 28 feet

TAKHLAKH LAKE CAMPGROUND

Randle, Washington

Just imagine: you're sitting in your campsite at Takhlakh Lake gazing out at a picture-perfect view of Mount Adams. It seems near enough to reach out and add a little more white here, a little more blue there with a paintbrush. A living canvas right at your fingertips.

If you've forgotten your paint set, however, make sure you capture at least a scene or two on film. This is one of those spots that simply begs to be documented. On a calm and clear early morning, there can be two views of the mountain—the real-life one and the one that is a mirror reflection in the lake. Definitely worth a frame or two.

There is no easy way to get to Takhlakh, which is part of its appeal and makes it worthy of inclusion in this book. The confusing network of Forest Service roads can be downright irritating, too, if you don't have a good map of the area. I was beginning to feel like a rat in a maze after a while. It's a good idea to stop at the ranger station either in Randle to the north (the preferred route) or Trout Lake to the south. Pick up maps, trail information, and backcountry permits.

Don't expect views of Mount Adams along the way to guide you. Except for a few stellar vistas across open farmlands as you head north from Trout Lake, say good-bye to the

CAMPGROUND RATINGS

Beauty:	★★★★★
Site privacy:	★★
Site spaciousness:	★★★
Quiet:	★★★★★
Security:	★★★★
Cleanliness/upkeep:	★★★★
Insect control:	★★ (summer)
	★★★★ (fall)

There are many campground options in this lake-studded sector of Mount Adams' northwestern flank, but none are quite so breathtaking when the mountain is in view. It's hard to get to, but worth it.

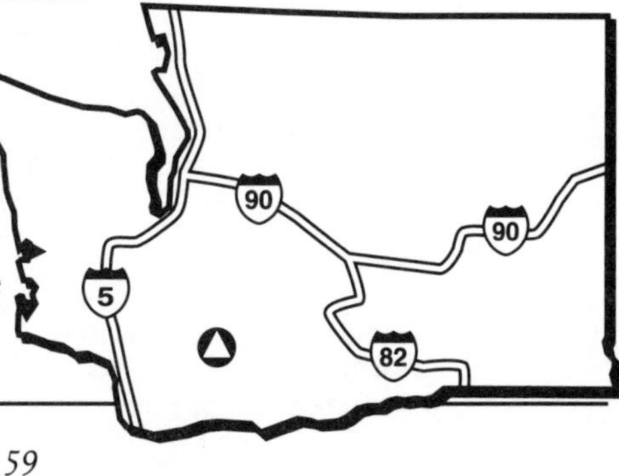

views until you are at lakeside. These are heavy alpine and subalpine timberlands of Gifford Pinchot National Forest. You don't want to spoil the surprise that awaits you at the lake, anyway. Besides, you'll be too busy making sure you're still on the right road (Forest Service Road 23) as it wends its way through dense stands of trees, deceptively gaining altitude until you reach Takhlakh Lake at 4,400 feet.

Most of the 54 tent sites offer views of the lake and the mountain through stands of Douglas fir, Engelmann spruce, pine, and subalpine fir. There is a campground host in attendance at Takhlakh (unusual for a campground so remotely situated but pleasant from a security standpoint), so anything you can't find, feel free to inquire.

If you've come in search of lazy fishing opportunities, Takhlakh is a treat. Only nonmotorized boats are allowed on the glassy waters. With an Ansel Adams–like scene at your back, cast your line, and wait for the trout lurking in the frigid glacial depths to find you.

For those with more ambitious recreational intentions, Mount Adams Wilderness is only minutes away. Trails lead ever higher as views of Washington's second highest volcano get better and better with every step. Wildflowers carpet the higher meadows with bursts of color throughout late spring and early summer. Birds are plentiful and diverse. Wildlife runs the gamut of deer, marmots, squirrels, chipmunks, bobcats, elk, and moose.

A section of the Pacific Crest National Scenic Trail passes Mount Adams on the western edge of the wilderness and is accessible from trailheads near

Takhlakh. Climbers also use these routes to reach Mount Adams' summit. It is possible to use Takhlakh as a base camp for extended forays around Mount Adams on what is known as the "Highline Trail." This is a rigorous navigation of 90% of the mountain. The last 10% would challenge even a mountain goat. Check with a ranger before tackling this.

While the spring and summer flower displays on Mount Adams can be inspiring, their loveliness can often be offset by an unwelcome accompaniment: mosquitoes. Although it varies from year to year, late summer and early fall are predictably the best times to avoid the pesky varmints altogether. I recommend the window of opportunity between late August and early October so you don't get caught in the crossfire (literally) of hunting season that follows soon after. Autumn colors make glorious photo opportunities in October, while the huckleberry season is usually at its peak by late August.

To get there from Randle, take County Road 3 off State Route 12 at Randle. Go south for 2 miles to FS 23. In another 29 miles, turn north onto FS 2329. The campground is a little over a mile in.

To get there from Trout Lake, take FS 80 north to its intersection with FS 23. The campground is nearly the same distance as from Randle, but the road twists and turns with vaguely marked intersections. The turnoff onto FS 2329 will be to the right coming from Trout Lake.

KEY INFORMATION

Takhlakh Lake Campground
c/o Gifford Pinchot National Forest
Randle Forest District
Randle, WA 98377

Operated by: Gifford Pinchot National Forest

Information: (360) 497-1100

Open: Mid-June through October, depending on snow

Individual sites: 54

Each site has: Picnic table, fire grill

Site assignment: First come, first served; no reservations

Registration: Not necessary

Facilities: Pit toilets, piped water, firewood, campground host

Parking: At individual sites

Fee: $9 per night

Elevation: 4,400 feet

Restrictions:

Pets–Permitted

Alcoholic beverages–Permitted

Vehicles– RVs and trailers up to 21 feet

Other–Nonmotorized boats only; backcountry permits required

WASHINGTON CAMPGROUNDS

EASTERN WASHINGTON

EAST

BROOKS MEMORIAL STATE PARK

Goldendale, Washington

In the early days of my short-lived career as a river rafting guide, I was part of the historic first commercial descent of the Klickitat River, a small, lively, and rapidly dropping tumble of water that courses off the slopes of Gilbert Peak high in the Goat Rocks Wilderness. Plunging south through the basalt-lined canyons of the Yakima Indian Reservation east of Mount Adams, the Klickitat finally succumbs to anonymity as it empties into the Columbia River at the small town of Lyle.

It was my dubious luck to hang around with a ragtag group of egocentric boaters who were always questing for the aqueous version of "steep and deep." You skiers know what I mean.

The Klickitat fit the bill—narrow, steep descents; nightmarish S-curves; boulder-strewn; and log-choked. To make a long story short, the river won. Klickitat—2, Ragtag Humiliated Group of Boaters—0.

Fortunately you'll find more than just hair-raising river running to keep you busy if you're in the Goldendale area and need a campground for the night.

From its 3,000-foot location in the Simcoe Mountains, Brooks Memorial State Park is not only a good base for exploring the Klickitat Valley, but also sights farther south to the Columbia River, west into the untamed Klickitat River region and Mount Adams, and north into the

CAMPGROUND RATINGS

Beauty:	★★★★★
Site privacy:	★★★
Site spaciousness:	★★★
Quiet:	★★★★★
Security:	★★★★
Cleanliness/upkeep:	★★★★★
Insect control:	★★★

Situated at roughly 3,000 feet in the Simcoe Mountains, Brooks Memorial makes for an excellent by-the-highway base camp for exploring the lovely scenery of the Klickitat Valley.

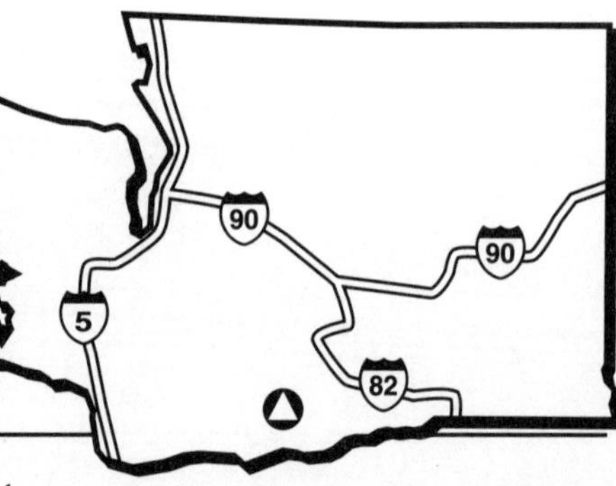

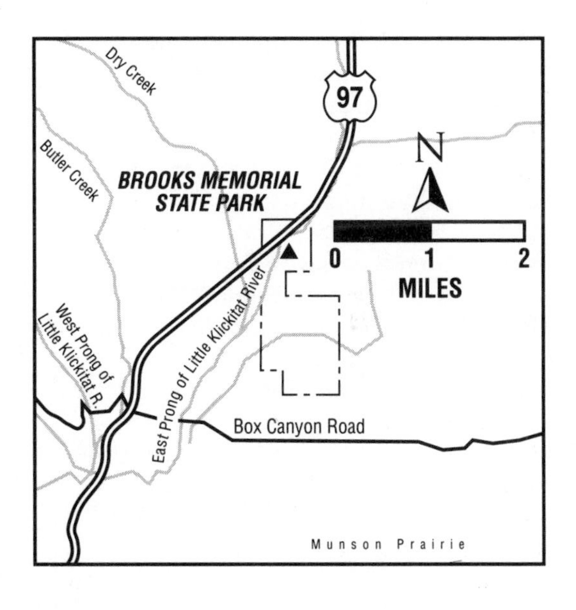

Yakima Indian Reservation and the viticultural lands of the Yakima Valley.

Points of interest abound in all directions. Central to the area is Goldendale, a quiet community that is home to the Goldendale Observatory State Park Interpretive Center and one of the largest telescopes available for public use in the country.

Down along the Columbia, historical attractions include Maryhill Museum and the American version of Stonehenge. Maryhill Museum houses the world-famous art collection of Sam—Who-in-the-Sam-Hill—Hill and his wife, Mary. Also the brainchild of Hill, the Stonehenge Memorial was created in the identical life-size dimensions of the original English formation to honor Klickitat County's young men who fought and died in World War I.

The entire area around Goldendale has had an active past. The Klickitat Indian tribe has inhabited the region for hundreds of years and was the instrumental negotiator between tribes from east and west who gathered in the region to trade and socialize. At Horsethief Lake State Park (on SR 14 along the Columbia), you can see Indian petroglyphs.

This is the dry side of the Cascades, which means hot and dry summers with cool nights. Winters are generally chilly and snowy. Brooks Memorial is open year-round and offers seasonal activities accordingly—hiking the park's trail system in summer, with cross-country skiing, snowmobiling, and snowshoeing in the winter.

Wildflowers bloom in the park from March until July, and there is quite a diversity of park wildlife—turkey, deer, raccoon, porcupine, beaver, bobcat, coyote, red-tailed hawk, and owl. The Little Klickitat River follows U.S. 97 from Brooks Memorial down into Goldendale, and it is not uncommon to observe beavers going about their business of damming the river.

Additional activities around Goldendale include golfing, windsurfing on the Columbia at Doug's Beach State Park, bicycling, and rock climbing.

Despite my tale of woe at the beginning of this chapter, river running is an option. Both the Klickitat and the White Salmon have their share of thrills and chills. The characteristics of both rivers make them best suited to kayak descents, but our pioneering rafting effort has led to continued popularity as well. Check out the local guide services for more information on this.

To get there from Yakima, follow U.S. 97 south for 55 miles, crossing Satus Pass (elevation 3,107 feet) to the park entrance.

KEY INFORMATION

Brooks Memorial State Park
2465 U.S. Highway 97
Goldendale, WA 98620

Operated by: Washington State Parks and Recreation Commission

Information: (509) 773-4611

Open: All year; limited winter facilities November through March

Individual sites: 45

Each site has: Picnic table, fire grill

Some sites have: Water and hookups for RVs

Site assignment: First come, first served; no reservations

Registration: Self-registration on site

Facilities: Restrooms with flush toilets, sinks, hot showers; public telephone; playground; primitive group camp; Environmental Learning Center for up to 104 people; firewood for sale; store within 1 mile

Parking: At campground and at individual sites

Fee: $10 standard per night; $15 hookup; $4 each additional vehicle

Elevation: Nearly 3,000 feet

Restrictions:

Pets–On leash

Fires–In fire pits; no firewood gathering

Alcoholic beverages–Permitted at campsite or picnic site

Vehicles–RVs up to 50 feet

FIELD'S SPRING STATE PARK

Anatone, Washington

Where the hell is Anatone?

Even if you're a born-and-bred native Washingtonian, you may have to reach for the map on this one. I'll give you a hint. If you've ever traveled between Clarkston and Enterprise (Oregon), you've driven right through Anatone. You probably blinked and missed it.

Needless to say, Anatone is quite small. But significant in the world of tent camping. It is the last stop for any kind of services before continuing on to Field's Spring State Park. That means that anything you need that they didn't have in Anatone is back the way you likely just came in Clarkston or Lewiston (Idaho). Beyond Field's Spring to the south lies wilderness, national forest, and wild river canyons. Maybe you better make one last check of that checklist.

Literally on the edge of nowhere (which is where most tent campers like to find themselves), Field's Spring State Park is actually a handy wilderness escape for folks from Clarkston and Lewiston (both about 20 miles away). For anyone else, the park is an ideal layover between destinations north and south or as a destination of its own. From the urban centers of western Washington and Oregon, it is easily an eight-hour drive. Admittedly, it is well off the beaten path, but that is part of its

CAMPGROUND RATINGS

Beauty:	★★★★★
Site privacy:	★★★
Site spaciousness:	★★★★★
Quiet:	★★★★
Security:	★★★★
Cleanliness/upkeep:	★★★★★
Insect control:	★

A handy wilderness escape from Clarkston and Lewiston, an ideal layover between destinations north and south, or a destination of its own.

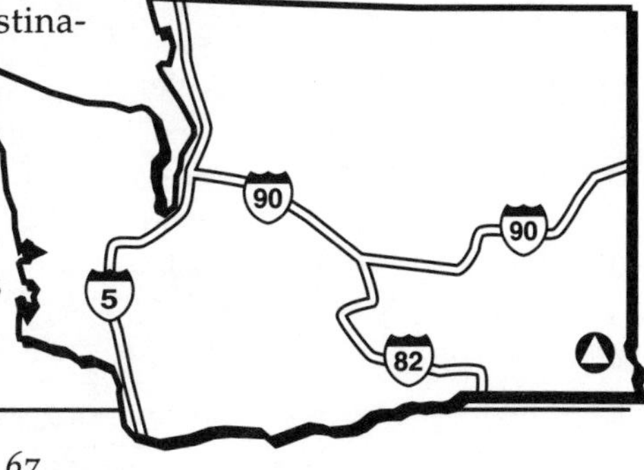

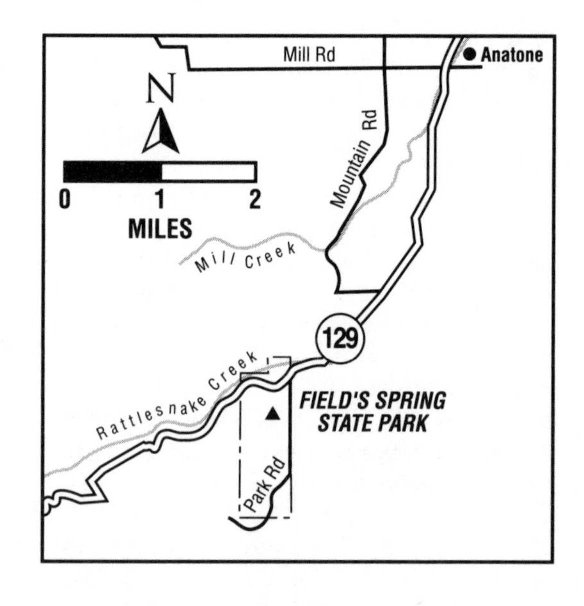

appeal. Besides, the roads are good all the way there. When the next long holiday weekend comes up, here's one to consider.

Sitting on a basalt foundation at 4,000 feet on the eastern edge of Washington's Blue Mountains, Field's Spring State Park is open all year and plays host to activities in every season. It is a place of unusual beauty in an otherwise harsh and rugged terrain, created by one of the largest and deepest lava flows in the world's geologic history. Evidence of this massive, recurring lava activity, known as the Columbia Plateau, can be best seen in the walls of river gorges and canyons throughout southeast Washington.

One of the best places to view the canyons themselves is right at the state park. A one-mile hike up Puffer Butte (elevation gain of 500 feet) provides vistas into both the Grande Ronde River and the mighty Snake River canyons and across the three states of Washington, Oregon, and Idaho, which come together in this corner. While the Snake River is practically a household word with its immensely popular boating adventures, the Grande Ronde enjoys relative obscurity as it wanders northeast out of Oregon's Anthony Lakes region. Of its total 185 miles, the Washington stretch of the Grande Ronde is mostly a drift trip with Class II and III rapids. It is not considered a highly technical river, but deceptively powerful eddies during high water and rocks at low periods require experienced skills.

Paddlers looking for greater technical challenges should venture upstream into the Oregon sector. The river has a Wild and Scenic designation on parts of its Oregon flow, and there are several put-in spots not far from Field's Spring. Take a good road map of the area if you plan to do any shuttling.

Escaping the heat of the summer is one of the biggest draws to Field's Spring. Although the park sits on what is essentially an arid, desert-like plateau with prickly pear cactus growing down along the Grande Ronde's banks, the difference in elevation makes all the difference in temperature. While Clarkston and Lewiston swelter in 100-degree agony in midsummer, Field's Spring rarely gets above a tolerable 85.

However, in winter this becomes somewhat the reverse. Snowy conditions make for ideal cross-country ski outings, and the park staff maintains 15 kilometers of trails.

In springtime catch the spectacular wildflower display or see if you can identify all eight different species of woodpeckers that nest in and among stands of western larch, grand fir, Douglas fir, and ponderosa pine that shade the campsites.

Field's Spring is a true oasis in a region otherwise parched for camping options.

To get there from Clarkston (roughly 110 miles south of Spokane), follow SR 129 south through Asotin and Anatone for about 25 miles to the park entrance.

KEY INFORMATION

Field's Spring State Park
P.O. Box 37
Anatone, WA 99401

Operated by: Washington State Parks and Recreation Commission

Information: (509) 256-3332

Open: All year

Individual sites: 20

Each site has: Picnic table, fire pit with grill, shade trees

Site assignment: First come, first served; no reservations

Registration: Self-registration on site

Facilities: Bathhouse with sinks, toilets, showers (25¢), hot water; public telephone; firewood; playground; limited disabled access; Environmental Learning Center with 2 lodges for group rental; store, restaurant, and ice nearby

Parking: At individual sites

Fee: $10 per night

Elevation: 4,000 feet

Restrictions:

Pets–On leash

Fires–In fire pits only

Alcoholic beverages–Permitted

Vehicles–No accommodations for RVs or trailers

GOOSE LAKE CAMPGROUND

Trout Lake, Washington

CAMPGROUND RATINGS

Beauty:	★★★★
Site privacy:	★★★★
Site spaciousness:	★★★★★
Quiet:	★★★★★
Security:	★★★★
Cleanliness/upkeep:	★★★★
Insect control:	★★ (summer)
	★★★★ (rest of year)

Put this one on your August and September list. The mosquitoes are a nightmare earlier in the season.

It would be a cruel hoax to lead you into the splendid alpine world of Indian Heaven Wilderness without giving you the bad news early on.

Just when the wildflowers are beginning their riotous displays of color, the snow has receded from all but the uppermost hiking trails, and daytime temperatures are warming to shirt-sleeve conditions, an insidious presence prevails that is the nightmare of midsummer mountain trekkers throughout much of the Northwest.

In a word, mosquitoes.

You laugh. What are a few harmless bugs? you ask. Well, we're not talking about the occasional little devil that wanders into your tent just as you're about to doze off and decides to make a snack of your forehead.

No, we're talking about droves. Swarms. Squadrons. Plague-sized packs. There is absolutely no relief from them when they are at their worst. Even a good insect repellent is often useless because it's more than just their bloodthirsty zeal that gets under your skin (pun intended). It's the incessant whining that can drive you straight out of the hills and into the sanctity of the nearest motel room. In my estimation, these winged fiends have been the cause of more ruined vacations than any other

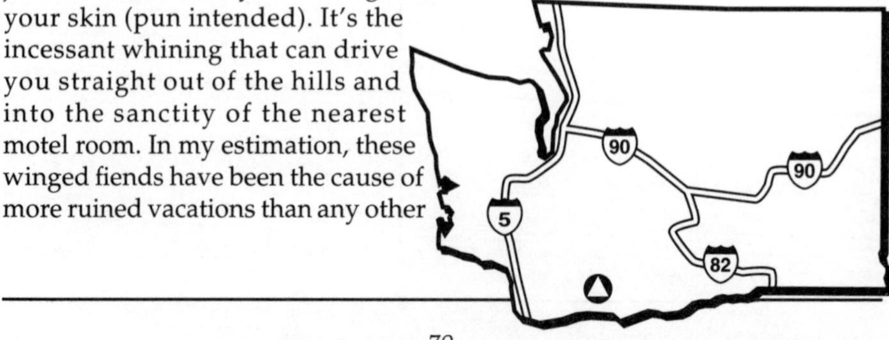

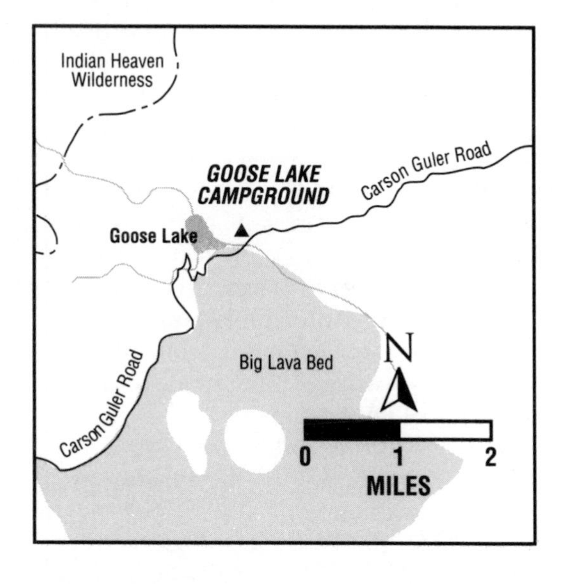

factor (except for domestic quarrels).

So armed with this knowledge, you may decide to put Goose Lake Campground on your August and September list of places to visit. Besides fewer mosquitoes, the higher altitudes offer bountiful huckleberries at this time of year, and the scenery is certainly no less spectacular. Fall colors, for example, peak in late September.

Goose Lake Campground sits at 3,200-foot elevation on FS 6035 about 13 miles southwest of Trout Lake. The ranger station for the Mount Adams District of Gifford Pinchot National Forest is in Trout Lake. It manages the areas around Goose Lake, including Indian Heaven Wilderness and a strange area known as Big Lava Bed. Pick up road maps, trail guides, and lots of other useful information at the ranger station in order to get the most out of your trip.

The campground is a tent camper's delight, with 25 tent sites and only one site large enough to accommodate an RV or trailer. The shortage of trailer sites is primarily due to the fact that the access road is very narrow and doesn't lend itself to passage by large or wide vehicles.

There is a boat ramp on the lake, and regular stocking with rainbow trout means good eating over the campstove. Many of the lakes in Indian Heaven Wilderness are planted with cutthroat trout.

If your interests lean toward the archaeological, Indian Heaven is a place for unique study. This high, rolling bench area between volcanoes (explosive Mount St. Helens to the northwest and Mount Adams to the northeast) once attracted Native American Indian tribes from as far away as Umatilla and

Warm Springs in Oregon. Its 175 lakes, beautiful meadows, and abundant wildlife provided the Indians with plentiful hunting, fishing, and berry-picking. They also indulged in one of their favorite sports in an area called the Indian Race Track. Faint sections of the track are still evident today and can be seen along the southern boundary of the wilderness between Red Mountain and Berry Mountain.

For the geology buff, Goose Lake sits on the northern edge of the eerie Big Lava Bed. This is a scene right out of a moonscape. Early volcanic eruptions produced a lava flow that hardened over 12,000 acres, leaving craters, caves, lava tubes, and other odd-shaped rock formations. The Forest Service warns that Big Lava Bed has few trails and is steep and rugged in places. If you bushwhack into the interior, keep in mind that magnetism emanating from all the rock surrounding you can affect the accuracy of your compass.

Toward Trout Lake, Ice Caves is another unusual volcanic formation worthy of exploration.

To get there from White Salmon on the Columbia River, drive north on SR 141 to Trout Lake (22 miles). Continue on SR 141 as it turns southwest and becomes FS 24 (Carson Guler Road) at about 5 miles. In another 2.5 miles, find FS 60 and go approximately 5 miles to the campground.

KEY INFORMATION

Goose Lake Campground
c/o Mount Adams Ranger District
Trout Lake, WA 98650

Operated by: Gifford Pinchot National Forest

Information: (509) 395-2501

Open: Mid-June to late September, depending on weather

Individual sites: 25 tent sites; 1 trailer site

Each site has: Picnic table, fire grill

Site assignment: First come, first served; reservations accepted

Registration: Not necessary

Facilities: Pit toilets, firewood, boat ramp

Parking: At individual sites

Fee: $6; $4 each additional vehicle

Elevation: 3,200 feet

Restrictions:

Pets–On leash

Fires–In fire pits only

Alcoholic beverages–In campsite only

Vehicles–Room for 1 trailer up to 18 feet

Other–No piped water

HAAG COVE CAMPGROUND

Kettle Falls, Washington

Set on the shore of Lake Roosevelt, against the sprawling backdrop of Colville National Forest—a 1,095,368-acre parcel in central northeastern Washington—Haag Cove is one of thirty-two campgrounds within the magnificent Coulee Dam National Recreation Area managed by the National Park Service.

The irony of Haag Cove's exquisite setting amidst towering ponderosa pine and Douglas fir is that its existence depends on a purely manmade landmark.

Lake Roosevelt is actually the flooded waters of the Columbia River. It was created when the monolithic Grand Coulee Dam was built in 1941 to harness the free-flowing power of the Columbia.

While you won't find the hundreds of salmon that used to attract Indians at Kettle Falls, there are 30 other species of game fish that make Lake Roosevelt a popular angling destination. You'll need a Washington State license, which you can pick up at area marinas or hardware and sporting goods stores. If you are unfamiliar with the territory, you may want to stop at the visitor center in Kettle Falls for informative brochures and maps.

Boats of every shape and size, motorized and unmotorized, ply the waters of Lake Roosevelt. With 660 miles of shoreline, there's plenty of room for everyone. But if you plan to do some boating, be advised of the

CAMPGROUND RATINGS

Beauty:	★★★★★
Site privacy:	★★★★
Site spaciousness:	★★★★★
Quiet:	★★★★★
Security:	★★★
Cleanliness/upkeep:	★★★★
Insect control:	★★★

A 130-mile-long lake at your feet. Mountains with the highest pass in Washington State at your back. Miles and miles of national forest lands to explore. An abundant diversity of wildlife to observe and photograph. The rich, cultural heritage of an Indian nation nearby.

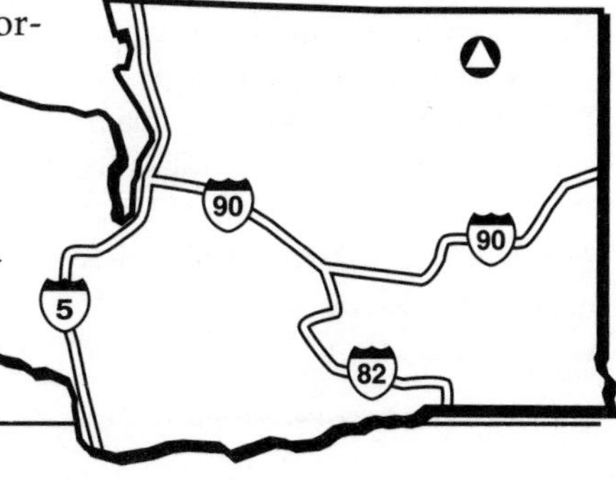

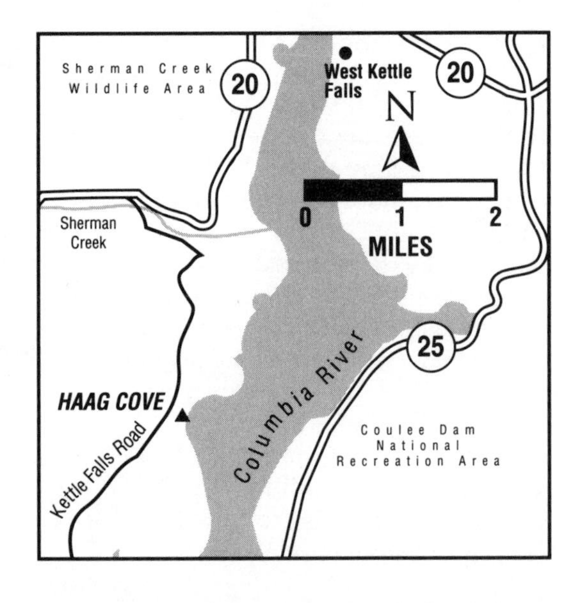

dos and don'ts on this particular body of water. Lake level varies according to season. It is lowered as much as 100 feet in the wintertime, but an interesting outing on land can be to walk the lake's exposed shoreline.

Despite man's capricious rendering of the region's contours, there is very much a sense of an unspoiled environment in this rugged, barren landscape. Deep canyons, sagebrush hills, and forested mountains are home to many varieties of animal and bird populations. One of the best spots for observing and shooting (with a camera) is just north of Haag Cove in Sherman Creek Habitat Management Area. Besides being a pretty area to explore, these 8,000 acres of land are protected by the Washington Department of Game for deer as a winter habitat and for other mammals all year.

The confluence of Sherman Creek and Lake Roosevelt produces a quality fly-fishing spot. The only other campground in the vicinity is Sherman Creek. However, it is boat-in only, one of the few campgrounds in eastern Washington accessible only by boat.

Hiking options are plentiful and relatively uncrowded in Colville National Forest. A gentler terrain, drier climate, and longer season compared to the Cascade area make for ideal conditions into the backcountry here. Sherman Pass, to the west on SR 20, is the high-altitude start (5,575 feet) for trails north and south into the Kettle River Range. Across Lake Roosevelt to the east is Huckleberry Range. Check with the Kettle Falls Ranger District for trail information.

Generally, the climate is warm and dry in summer months, with daytime temperatures ranging between 75° and 100°. Temperatures drop to between 50° and 60° at night. Spring and fall are cooler but still dry and very pleasant. Eastern Washington winters vary but can often be cold and snowy. Since Haag Cove is open all year, check current weather conditions if you plan an off-season outing. Remember, Sherman Pass is the highest in the state and may prove impassable in bad weather.

A number of self-guided driving tours and scenic routes not far from Haag Cove offer another perspective of Coulee Dam country. Bangs Mountain Loop, for example, takes you through stands of old-growth ponderosa pine. Historical points of interest at Fort Spokane and in Kettle Falls can be combined with a lovely drive on Route 25, which parallels Lake Roosevelt on the east side.

To get there from Kettle Falls (81 miles northwest of Spokane), drive west on SR 20 across this upper portion of the Columbia River, stay on SR 20 as it turns south along the river to the turnoff for Inchelium-Kettle Falls Road at about 7 miles. Take Inchelium-Kettle Falls Road south for 5 miles to the campground.

KEY INFORMATION

Haag Cove Campground
c/o Kettle Falls Ranger District
Route 1, Box 537
Kettle Falls, WA 99141

Operated by: Coulee Dam National Recreation Area

Information: (509) 633-9441

Open: All year

Individual sites: 18

Each site has: Picnic table, fire grill

Site assignment: First come, first served; no reservations

Registration: Not necessary

Facilities: Piped water, pit toilets, boat dock

Parking: At individual sites

Fee: $10 per night, May to October only

Elevation: 2,500 feet

Restrictions:

Pets–On leash

Fires–In fire pits only

Alcoholic beverages–Permitted in campsite

Vehicles–RVs or trailers up to 26 feet

Other–Fishing license required; boat launch permit required; 7-day permit is $6, 1-year permit is $30

HARTS PASS CAMPGROUND

Mazama, Washington

Mention the name, Harts Pass, to just about anyone who considers himself or herself a well-traveled outdoor adventurer in the Northwest, and watch their eyes glaze over.

When I was asking for campground suggestions in the North Cascades, I got as many different choices as the number of people I asked. Except that they would always end by saying (almost as an afterthought so they wouldn't risk offending me), with a cautious sidelong glance, "Of course, you've already got Harts Pass?" Something between a question and a statement.

For those of you who thought you were keeping your magical place to yourself, I'm sorry. You probably won't be alone on your next outing there. However, there are enough peaks and meadows and forests and trails in just about every direction you look that discovering a special spot all to yourself is at least half the fun of rambling these heady altitudes so classically prototypical of North Cascades terrain.

For starters, Harts Pass Campground sits on the western edge of the massive Pasayten Wilderness, a 505,524-acre tract that extends north to the Canadian border. Within this territory are 1,000 miles of trails, many of them without maintenance and leading into some of the

CAMPGROUND RATINGS

Beauty:	★★★★★
Site privacy:	★★★
Site spaciousness:	★★★
Quiet:	★★★★★
Security:	★★★
Cleanliness/upkeep:	★★★★
Insect control:	★

Remote and spectacularly beautiful, this small tents-only campground is an outdoor adventurer's dream. Get there before the snow!

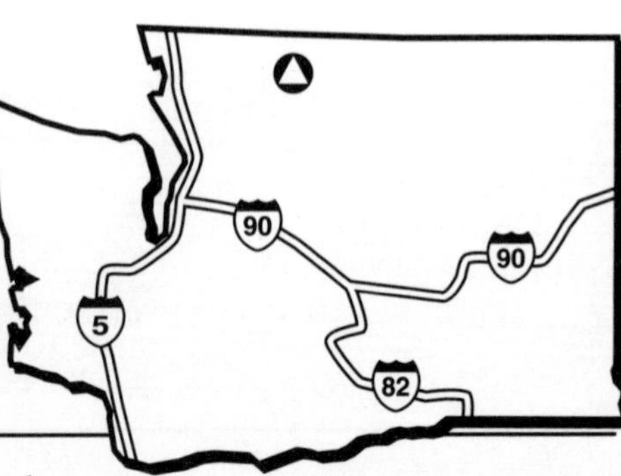

most difficult topography in the entire Washington Cascade range. Out of the metamorphic rock, Ice Age glaciers have produced an intimidating collection of razorlike ridges, deep valley troughs, cirques, and couloirs that tests the most skilled mountaineers.

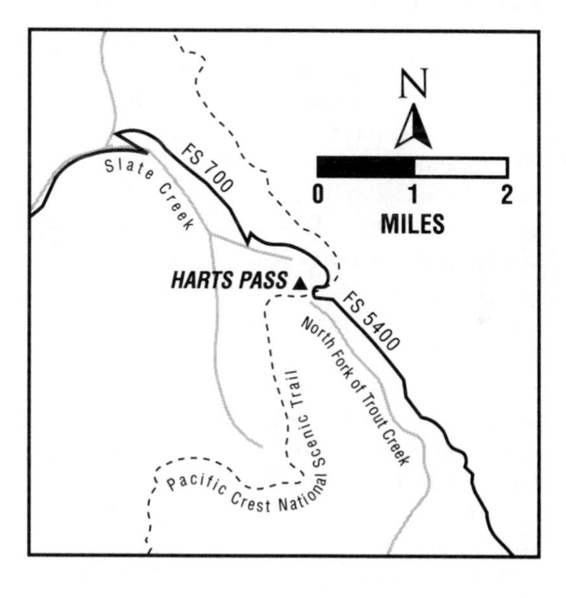

If you're not quite up to tackling nature at its rugged best, try a simpler approach with a drive up to Slate Peak Lookout. This is the highest point in Washington State accessible by car. Once one of ninety-three manned Forest Service lookouts in the North Cascade range, Slate Peak (at 7,440 feet) offers identification displays of the endless peaks, passes, and ridges visible from its 360-degree viewing area.

Passing near camp, the Pacific Crest National Scenic Trail is the major north-south thoroughfare for foot travel. It can be followed in either direction for further sampling of North Cascade beauty. Wide meadows burst with nearly six dozen flowering varieties of plant life at the height of their bloom (at this altitude and latitude, that tends to be late July to mid-August).

The road into Harts Pass from Mazama (a tedious 13 miles) is not recommended for extra-wide or low-clearance vehicles. For those of you daring enough to continue beyond Harts Pass by car, there are some points of historical interest to reward your perseverance. I'll warn you now: The road gets even rougher down into the Slate Creek valley where evidence of mining activity from the 1880s and 1890s still lingers. Down the road from

Chancellor, en route to Barron, is an abandoned building that once served as the stage stop and post office for the mining community before the Harts Pass road was built. If you can get there, the area around Chancellor and Barron is worth investigation.

A word of caution about traveling into these remote North Cascade destinations: Mazama offers little in the way of services, and there is really nothing substantial between Winthrop to the east on Highway 20 and Marblemount to the west—a stretch of 100 spectacularly scenic but civilization-free miles.

Despite its ranking as one of the ten most scenic drives in the United States, North Cascades Highway is not kept open year-round. It is usually the first of the east-west highways to close due to heavy snowfall (normally November to April). You may want to beat the snow with an early fall camping trip to Harts Pass just to take in the lovely autumn colors that will escort you the entire way. If you're thinking of going right after the snowmelt, keep in mind that the mosquitoes and horseflies will then be at their worst.

If you find accommodations at Harts Pass a bit tight (there are only five tent sites), try Meadows Campground (14 sites) a mile from the turnoff at FS 5400 down FS 500.

To get there from Mazama (about 15 miles northwest of Winthrop just off SR 20), follow Mazama Road (Lost Creek Road) for about 6 miles to FS 5400. The campground is 12 slow miles down FS 5400.

KEY INFORMATION

Harts Pass Campground
c/o Winthrop Ranger District
Box 579
Winthrop, WA 98862

Operated by: Okanogan National Forest

Information: (509) 996-2266

Open: Mid-July to late September

Individual sites: 5

Each site has: Picnic table

Site assignment: First come, first served; no reservations

Registration: Not necessary

Parking: In campground

Fee: No fee

Elevation: 6,198 feet

Restrictions:

Pets–On leash

Fires–No fires

Alcoholic beverages–Permitted

Vehicles–No RVs or trailers

LAKE WENATCHEE STATE PARK

Leavenworth, Washington

Although it is quite large, Lake Wenatchee State Park is a pretty nice spot with spacious and secluded campsites and oodles of choices for enjoying the outdoor recreation of one of Washington State's most scenic and untainted areas.

Within easy access of Lake Wenatchee are Forest Service roads leading to two of the largest and most ruggedly beautiful designated wildernesses—Alpine Lakes Wilderness to the south across State Route 2 and Glacier Peak Wilderness to the northwest. There are miles of trails that network throughout both areas and into such spectacular high country that choosing a route to fit into your time schedule can be a monumental task. There are any number of backpacking options that deserve at least a week's time.

Both wildernesses and all of the area surrounding Lake Wenatchee are part of the massive Wenatchee National Forest (2,200,000 acres), which stretches along the eastern crest of the Cascade Mountains from Lake Chelan south to Yakima Indian Reservation.

Many thousands of years ago, the eastern edge of the subcontinent merged with the existing North American continent in a crush of ancient metamorphosed rock. Granite intruded at various times, and a newer cap of volcanic debris settled over the scene. The

CAMPGROUND RATINGS

Beauty:	★★★★★
Site privacy:	★★★
Site spaciousness:	★★★ (South campground) ★★★★ (North campground
Quiet:	★★★
Security:	★★★★
Cleanliness/upkeep:	★★★★
Insect control:	★

Here's one for the entire family. It's got everything!

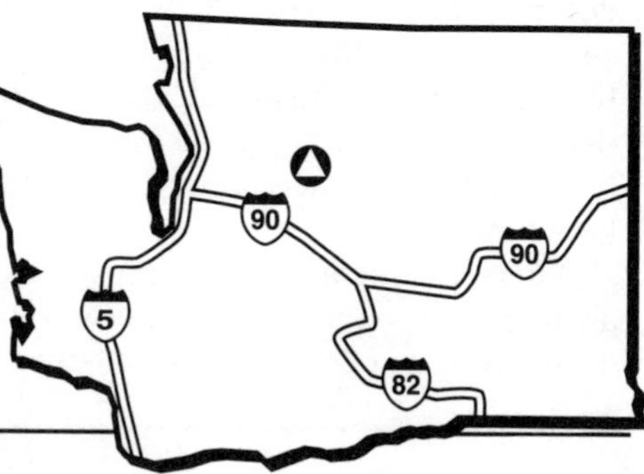

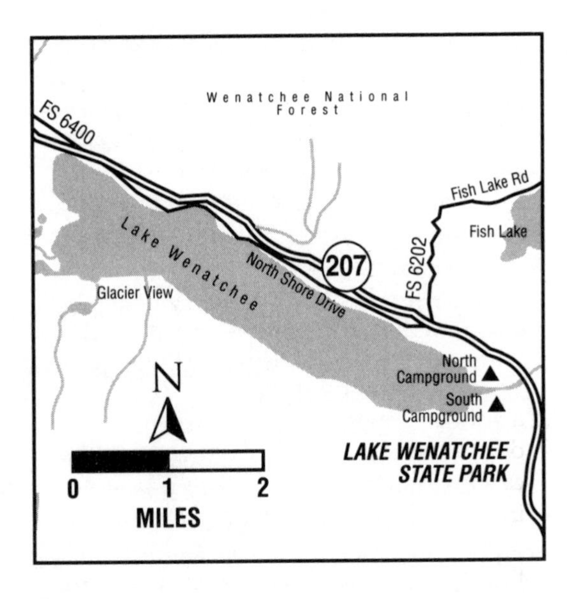

resultant topography in much of the national forest is an odd mixture of steeply upthrusting ridges with rivers falling in between, carving narrow canyons.

Lake Wenatchee itself is the source of the Wenatchee River, fed by the glaciers of Glacier Park (the largest active collection in the continental United States). Numerous boating options are available on both Lake Wenatchee and the Wenatchee River. Canoes can be rented at the park's concession stand. Chances are you'll be sharing the waters with an assortment of other craft, ranging from fishermen in rowboats and motorized dinghies to kayaks, windsurfing boards, and maybe even a raft or two.

Past the crashing torrent of Tumwater Canyon (where you can occasionally get a glimpse of lunatic kayakers having the ride of their lives) and just east of the Bavarian-style burg of Leavenworth, the Wenatchee River becomes the most heavily rafted and kayaked stretch of water in the state. I got my whitewater–guide wings on this run, just like almost every other certified guide this side of Stevens Pass. It's a 21-mile potpourri of everything from lazy flatwater floats to rollicking Class IV hydraulics. Some books list a few of the rapids at Class VI! It is best—no, make that MANDATORY—to go with a commercial outfit unless you are an accomplished boater and know the river.

Otherwise, recreational opportunities span the seasons at Lake Wenatchee as the park is open year-round (with limited winter facilities). Fishing is one of the most popular summer pastimes, while autumn brings travelers into the area for the glorious display of changing colors and Leavenworth's lively Oktoberfest. In winter, snows can be heavy, and the park maintains a respectable number of trails for cross-country skiers and snowmobilers. Springtime is a lovely chance to see the apple, peach, pear, and cherry orchards of the Wenatchee Valley in full bloom. Come back at harvesttime for some sampling.

Lake Wenatchee State Park is a sprawling 489-acre complex divided into North and South campgrounds. The sites are available on a first come, first served basis, and if you can manage it, go for the sites in the northern section. They're closer to the river and more spacious.

On this eastern slope of the Cascades, summers are hot and dry. Thunderstorms materialize out of nowhere, and lightning strikes can quickly ignite the forests in late summer and early fall. Be aware of the fire danger at all times, and don't throw matches or cigarette butts carelessly. Make sure they land squarely in a fire pit that's about to be doused.

Also be aware that this is bear country. Food should be stored in the car when not being consumed; a tent is not much of a deterrent to a hungry bear.

To get there from Leavenworth (23 miles west of Wenatchee), take U.S. 2 west for 16 miles to SR 207. The state park and campground are 5 miles up SR 207.

KEY INFORMATION

Lake Wenatchee State Park
21588A Highway 207
Leavenworth, WA 98826

Operated by: Washington State Parks and Recreation Commission

Information: (509) 763-3101 or (800) 233-0321

Open: April through September 30; with limited facilities October through March

Individual sites: 197

Each site has: Fire pit and grill, picnic table, shade trees

Site assignment: First come, first served; no reservations

Registration: Self-registration on site

Facilities: Centrally located comfort stations with hot showers, toilets, sinks; store, firewood, public telephone, restaurant, playground; boat launch, boat rentals; group camp; horseback riding; campfire programs; nature walks; junior ranger programs; limited disabled access

Parking: At individual sites

Fee: $11 per night; $5 each additional vehicle

Elevation: 1,866 feet

Restrictions:

Pets–On leash

Fires–In fire pits; seasonal restrictions based on fire hazard conditions; no gathering of firewood

Alcoholic beverages–In campsites or at picnic sites

Vehicles–No RV hookups

SILVER FALLS CAMPGROUND

Entiat, Washington

This listing comes highly endorsed by a number of sources, including the manager of the state parks at Lake Chelan. That should tell you something. About Lake Chelan, at least.

In the summer, this second-deepest lake in the United States is a tourist and vacationer's mecca for just about every variety of outdoor recreation you can imagine. Campgrounds are at overflow stage week after week.

This is not to take anything away from the spectacular beauty of the place. Unfortunately, this is the wry irony of so many places in the Northwest. Their singular and stunning scenery is what attracts people in the first place. Sometimes the enthusiasm gets out of hand, as in the case of Lake Chelan, in my opinion. If you can look beyond the cluster of lakeside resorts and condominiums and RV parks that mar the southern stretches of the shoreline, however, the natural splendor of the 55-mile-long, glacier-fed lake with mountain slopes rising as high as 8,000 feet and blanketed in aspen, cottonwood, fir, and pine is what you will see.

Silver Falls Campground sits deep in the canyon-gouged Entiat River Valley in isolated splendor amidst stands of cottonwoods, pine, fir, and aspen. The Entiat River and Silver Creek meet at the campground, and a trail leads one-half

CAMPGROUND RATINGS

Beauty:	★★★★★
Site privacy:	★★★★★
Site spaciousness:	★★★★
Quiet:	★★★★★
Security:	★★★★
Cleanliness/upkeep:	★★★★
Insect control:	★★★

The Lake Chelan area, while spectacularly beautiful, is overrun with tourists; but not far away lies this uncrowded, overlooked escape.

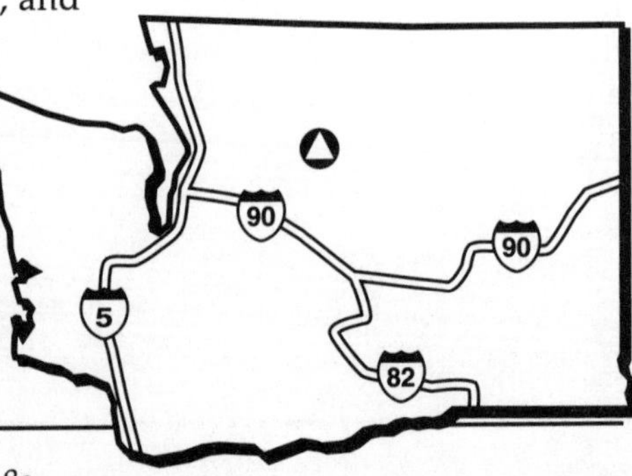

mile to the base of lovely Silver Falls. Other trailheads into the Entiat and Chelan Mountains are a short drive from the campground. At road's end (nearly 40 miles from the main highway) is another Forest Service campground and a trailhead into the wild and remote southern portions of Glacier Peak Wilderness. This is terrain for experienced backpackers only because it has steep, grueling ascents over trails of crumbling, ancient, volcanic rock. At least half-a-dozen peaks above Entiat Meadows are in the 7,000- to 8,000-foot range. This is the eastern edge of the Cascade Mountains, where vegetation is not as dense as the western side. Trails often traverse dry, sun-parched routes. Carry water from midsummer on, and be aware that thunderstorms can be sudden and fierce.

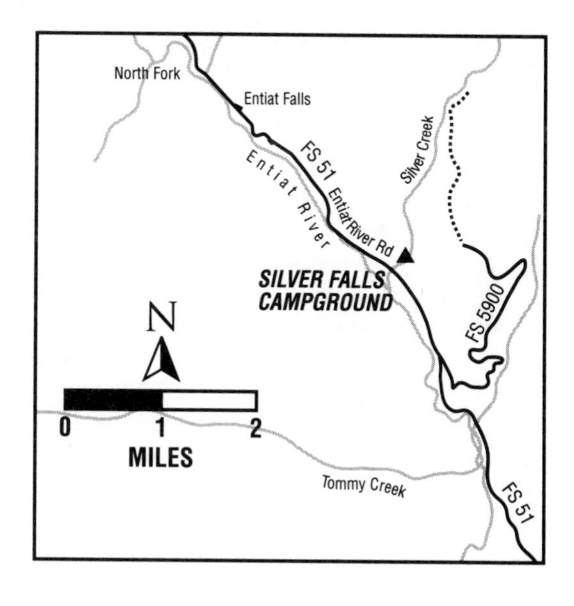

Coming up to Silver Falls from the town of Entiat is a contrast to the landscape higher up. Fed by a glacier of the same name, Entiat River and its innumerable small tributaries are part of the water supply for a small but thriving apple orchard industry that got its start through the perseverance of a Caribbean farmer who settled in the Entiat Valley in 1868. His first attempts with peaches and prunes failed miserably. Apples were tried not long after, and the rest is history. The apple industry in Washington State today is one of the state's most lucrative industries.

Continuing deeper into the valley, the terraced orchards give way to the coolness of pine and cottonwood forests, with the grandeur of the rugged peaks providing a dramatic backdrop higher up. Looking back, the rich blue-green of the Columbia, the lush assortment of fruit orchards on the benchlands, and the dry, rolling wheat-fields of the eastern plateau are, in a single eyeful, visual components of the diversity that Washington State offers to travelers.

In addition to Silver Falls, Preston Falls and Entiat Falls are worthwhile sidetrips. Take a peek down into Box Canyon from the marked viewpoint. Mountain bikers will enjoy the network of Forest Service roads into the Entiat Valley, but be reminded that wheeled vehicles are not allowed in designated wilderness areas.

Those of you who can't resist the siren song of civilization nearby, can sneak off the back way to Lake Chelan via FS 5900 (Shady Pass Road) and be back at camp by nightfall. Take the main highway out of Chelan on your return route for a full-loop trip. The drive is quite lovely coming out of Knapp Coulee on a mild summer evening as the setting sun casts its glow over the Columbia River in the rosy and golden hues of peach and apple country.

To get there from Wenatchee, drive north on US Alt. 97 for about 15 miles to Entiat River Road (just south of the town of Entiat). Turn left (west) onto Entiat River Road (FS 51) and drive 30 miles to the campground.

KEY INFORMATION

Silver Falls Campground
c/o Entiat Ranger District
P.O. Box 476, 2108 Entiat Way
Entiat, WA 98822

Operated by: U.S. Forest Service, Wenatchee National Forest, Entiat Ranger District

Information: (509) 784-1511

Open: Late May or early June through October, depending on snow

Individual sites: 31

Each site has: Fire ring, picnic table, shade trees

Site assignment: First come, first served; no reservations

Registration: Self-registration on site

Facilities: Pit toilets, centralized water pumps, disability accessible trail

Parking: In campground and at individual sites

Fee: $5 per vehicle per night

Elevation: 2,600 feet

Restrictions:

Pets–On leash

Fires–Restricted during dry seasons

Alcoholic beverages–Permitted

Vehicles–No ATVs in Wenatchee National Forest

OREGON CAMPGROUNDS

WESTERN OREGON

CAPE BLANCO STATE PARK

Port Orford, Oregon

We head briefly to the Pacific maritime climes for the next three campground installments in what I like to refer to as "the cape collection."

The first of them, Cape Blanco, is the farthest point south of the trio. The cape, the park, the reef, the lighthouse, the airport, and the road that leads from U.S.101 all bear the name given to the dramatic cliffs that rise for 200 feet above a black sand beach. In 1603 a relatively unknown Spanish explorer named Martin d'Aguilar spotted the sheer white ("blanco," to him) cliffs and aptly dubbed them for posterity.

The state park covers 1,895 acres of forested headlands and wildflower fields that flood the area with color in late spring and early summer. Yellow coneflowers, coral bells, yellow sand verbena, and northern dune tansy are the most prevalent varieties. The Sitka spruce dominates in the tree department. Farther east in the Coast Ranges, one can find old-growth Douglas fir and the commercially prized Port Orford cedar.

The lush vegetation of Cape Blanco is kept green by the year-round temperate marine climate that brings in half of the total annual precipitation between December and February. There's more rain and heavy fog from late October through mid-May, but summers (thank heavens!) are generally sunny and mild. It never really gets too hot or too cold.

CAMPGROUND RATINGS

Beauty:	★★★★★
Site privacy:	★★★
Site spaciousness:	★★★★
Quiet:	★★ (summer)
	★★★★★ (off-season)
Security:	★★★★
Cleanliness/upkeep:	★★★★★
Insect control:	★★★

Cape Blanco happens to be the westernmost point in Oregon and houses the most westerly lighthouse (historic Cape Blanco Light) on the United States mainland.

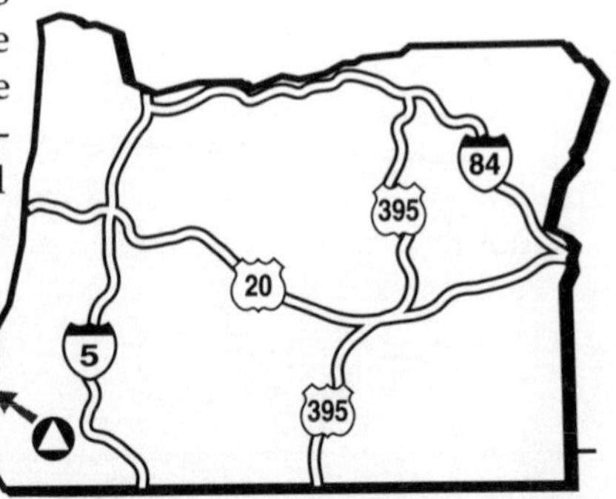

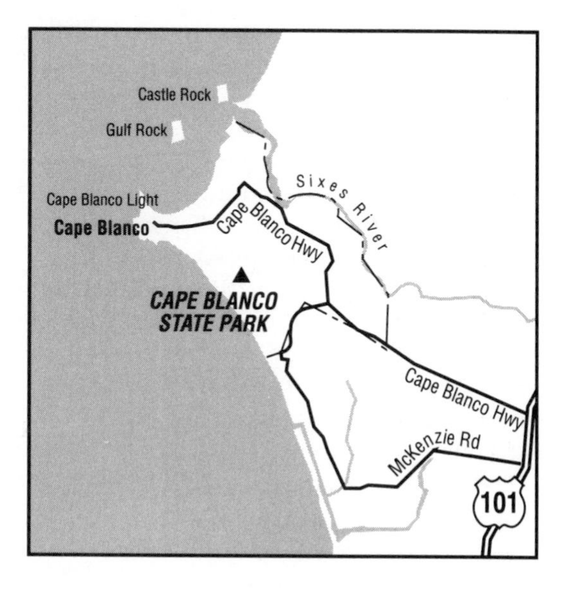

This makes it an ideal place to enjoy during the off-season and to avoid at peak times. The summer tourist season along the Oregon Coast—all 360 miles of it—is lovely weatherwise, and the scenery is consistently spectacular, but it is one of those experiences you could learn to hate. There is little relief from the crowds, campgrounds fill up quickly (including Cape Blanco, which doesn't require reservations), and the main north/south route (U.S. 101) is one long, nearly unbroken procession of RVs and trailers.

But if summer is the only time you can get there, by all means go. You just have to be a little more creative in finding those pockets of isolation. Joining the seals offshore in the string of craggy, black basalt outcroppings of Oregon Islands National Wildlife Refuge may be a bit extreme, however. That is what binoculars are for. Instead, try the New River paddle route just upcoast from the park in the town of Denmark. This 8-mile stretch of tidewater attracts shorebirds and migratory waterfowl to its shallow environs. The New River is a blend of fresh waters descending from Coast Ranges and the salty Pacific, creating an interesting estuarine mix. On one end of the river is undeveloped Floras Lake State Park, and at the other end are the sand dunes of Bandon. Both are equally worthy of exploration.

Another alternative is the Sixes River, which forms the northern boundary of Cape Blanco State Park. Fishing is best in the off-season in the Sixes—chinook in the fall, sea-run cutthroat trout in spring and fall, and steelhead in the winter. There are several boat put-ins along the river east of U.S. 101.

Restless foot wanderers can take their pick of hikes in varying topographies. A moderate climb up to the windswept bluff near the lighthouse offers views in all directions—north to Blacklock Point and Tower Rock, west across Blanco Reef, and south to Orford Reef. This is an excellent vantage point from which to watch gray whales on their migration path from the Arctic to Baja, California, in winter months.

Down on the beach, you can walk along portions of the Oregon Coast Trail, but keep in mind that tide levels change anywhere from 6 to 12 feet two times each day. For the ultimate escape for those of you experienced enough to handle it, Grassy Knob Wilderness lies not far east in a small section of Siskiyou National Forest. Travel through this area is best described as bushwhacking—there are very few established trails and the going is steep and rugged.

To get there from Port Orford, drive north on U.S. 101 to Cape Blanco Highway, and then go 5 miles west to the state park campground.

KEY INFORMATION

Cape Blanco State Park
P.O. Box 299
Sixes, OR 97476

Operated by: Oregon State Parks and Recreation

Information: (503) 332-2971

Open: Mid-April to late September

Individual sites: 58; separate hiker/biker camp

Each site has: Picnic table, fire grill

Some sites have: Shade trees

Site assignment: First come, first served; no reservations

Facilities: Bathhouse with sinks, toilets, hot showers; firewood; laundromat; some disabled access

Parking: At individual site

Fee: $11 per night for tent campers; slightly higher for RVs

Elevation: 200 feet

Restrictions:

Pets–On leash only

Fires–In fire pits only

Alcoholic beverages–Prohibited

Vehicles–No limit on RV size

CAPE LOOKOUT STATE PARK

Netarts, Oregon

Our second "cape camping" selection is the lovely and linear Cape Lookout State Park, just south of Netarts on the Three Capes Scenic Drive that encompasses two other magnificent headlands (Cape Meares on the north and Cape Kiwanda on the south). These are also state parks but are limited to day-use activities.

Collectively these three areas cover more than 2,500 acres of coastal rain forest, sheer cliffs, wide sandy beaches and dunes, narrow spits, rocky points and outcroppings, protected bays, and estuaries.

To accommodate the sizable numbers of seashore enthusiasts, the well-maintained and efficiently designed Cape Lookout State Park offers a whopping 194 tent sites that are accessible all year. In addition, it offers hikers and bikers a separate area not far from the central camping grounds. Group camps are also available, as well as a meeting hall.

You will undoubtedly be surprised to learn that many of the capes along the Oregon coast are the wind-, weather-, and wave-carved remains of ancient volcanoes. Geologists speculate that massive Cape Lookout, considered by many to be one of the most scenic capes in the Northwest, originally formed as an island off the coast when a huge lava flow cooled and congealed differently above and below sea level. You can observe the layers from the base of this 700-foot promontory.

CAMPGROUND RATINGS

Beauty:	★★★★★
Site privacy:	★★★★
Site spaciousness:	★★★
Quiet:	★★★ (summer)
	★★★★★ (winter)
Security:	★★★★
Cleanliness/upkeep:	★★★★★
Insect control:	★★★

Superb views, wildlife refuges, historic sites, and various other points of interest make Cape Lookout and surrounding environs a popular destination for weekenders and summer vacationers from Oregon's metropolitan areas.

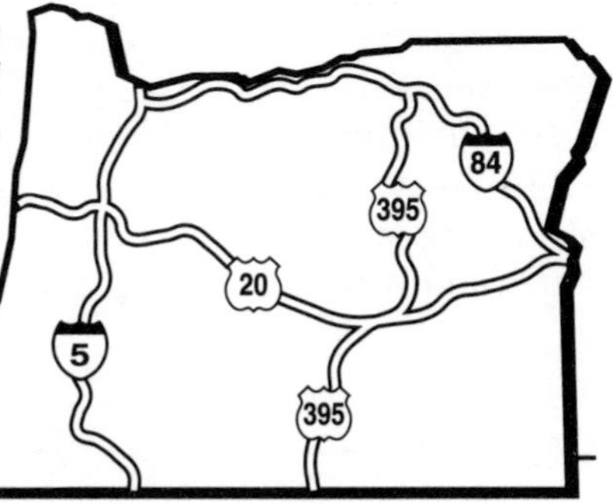

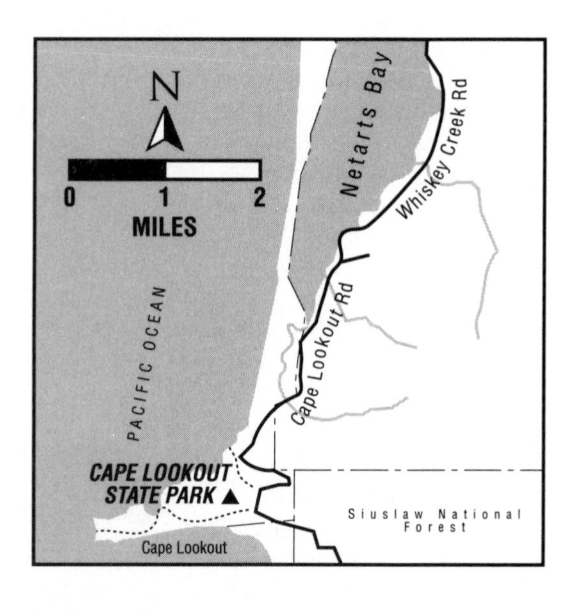

The Cape Meares formation occurred similarly.

Cape Kiwanda, however, is essentially compressed sand-into-rock that shoved upward. Its sandstone composition would normally make Cape Kiwanda a fragile target of the pounding surf, but as if by a master plan, nature provided the lofty point with its own Haystack Rock. (The more famous one is farther north, off the coast of Cannon Beach.) This giant piece of basalt encumbers incoming waves so effectively that fishermen in boats can head directly into the subdued breakers. Pacific City (south of Cape Kiwanda) holds the Pacific City Dory Derby each summer in honor of this, showing off the talents of its famous fleet of flat-bottomed boats.

The Cape Meares cliffs are the nesting grounds for a wide variety of shorebirds that are protected, along with their forest-dwelling counterparts, by Cape Meares National Wildlife Refuge and Three Arch Rock National Wildlife Refuge in Oceanside. Between the two refuges, over 150 species of birds are known to inhabit shores and uplands. Cape Meares is also the site of the "Octopus Tree," a Sitka spruce gone wild with an inordinate number of drooping branches. Tillamook Light, an historic lighthouse on Cape Meares, is another of the park's attractions.

The average 90 inches of annual rainfall keep things fairly wet in winter and struggling to dry out in summer. If you dress appropriately, hiking the headlands and watching storms roll in can be an exhilarating winter adventure along this stretch of Oregon coast. Keep in mind that trails are steep and slick in places. Safer and equally interesting is the 5-mile stroll along Cape Lookout State Park's sand spit, between the ocean and Netarts Bay.

In the bay's calm waters, you'll find conditions ideal for crabbing, either by boat or from the shore. Supplies can be found in town, and several places will cook your catch for you. Clamming and fishing are other options.

If you run out of things to do (which is unlikely) and want to play tourist, Tillamook is nearby. It has an historic museum and tours of its renowned cheese factory. If you're wondering about those huge aluminum barns out in the middle of a pasture, they house old dirigibles, relics of a bygone age of aviation. Unfortunately they are not open to the public.

To get there from Tillamook, drive southwest on Netarts Highway, and follow signs the entire way for Cape Lookout State Park. Total distance from Tillamook is about 10 miles without any detours or side trips.

KEY INFORMATION

Cape Lookout State Park
13000 Whiskey Creek Road West
Tillamook, OR 97141

Operated by: Oregon State Parks and Recreation

Information: (503) 842-3182

Open: All year

Individual sites: 251; separate hiker/biker camp

Each site has: Picnic table, fire pit and grill, piped water, shade trees

Site assignment: Reservations accepted, call (800) 452-5687, $6 fee; otherwise first come, first served

Registration: On site

Facilities: Bathhouse with flush toilets, sinks, hot water, showers; public telephone; day-use area just south of the hiker/biker camp has picnic tables, grills, a shelter and beach access; limited disabled access

Parking: At individual sites

Fee: $16 or $17 tent campers, $20 full hookup (summer); $13 or $14 tent campers, $15 or $17 full hookup (winter); $4 per person per day for hiker/biker sites (year round)

Elevation: Sea level

Restrictions:

Pets–On 6-foot leash

Alcoholic beverages–Permitted

CAPE PERPETUA SCENIC AREA

Yachats, Oregon

Perpetua was named by Captain James Cook in 1778 as he fearlessly continued north in that endless search for the Pacific link to the Northwest Passage. Both Cape Perpetua and the nearby town of Yachats (pronounced *yah hots*) have long been the vacation destination favored by Oregonians who choose the small town's relative seclusion amidst some of the coast's most awe-inspiring scenery. For some unknown reason, Yachats is often overlooked by tourists heading for the bustling centers of Newport and Florence, nearly equidistant to the north and south.

Long before tourists had a road to take them anywhere in this vicinity, however, the fog-shrouded seashore and mountain slopes were the domain of coastal Indian tribes who fished, clammed, and hunted in blissful obscurity. Their contentment was short-lived once the Spanish, English, and Germans discovered the rich resources awaiting exploitation. Along the coast and up verdant river valleys, timber mills, fish canneries, and dairy farms thrived from the late-18th century until the recent past. While there is still significant activity from these traditional industries, tourism has begun to replace them in the last several decades. Waning resources have forced residents of towns and villages all along the Oregon coast to consider alternative methods of

CAMPGROUND RATINGS

Beauty:	★★★★★
Site privacy:	★★
Site spaciousness:	★★★
Quiet:	★★★★
Security:	★★★★
Cleanliness/upkeep:	★★★★
Insect control:	★★★★

It may sound vaguely similar to Cape Lookout, but this is widely considered to be one of the Oregon coast's most spectacular headlands.

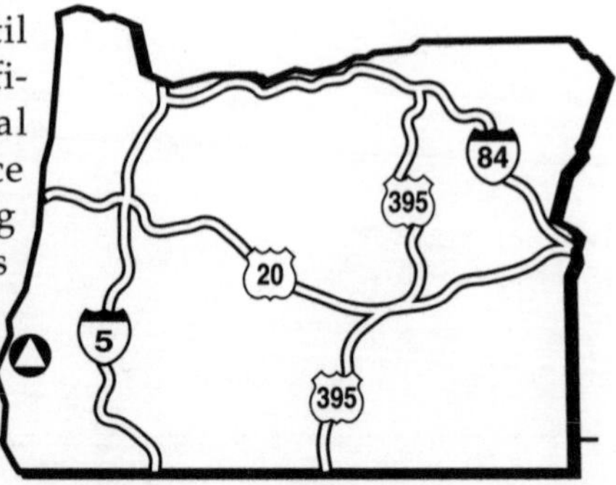

making a living. The transition has not been easy for many of them.

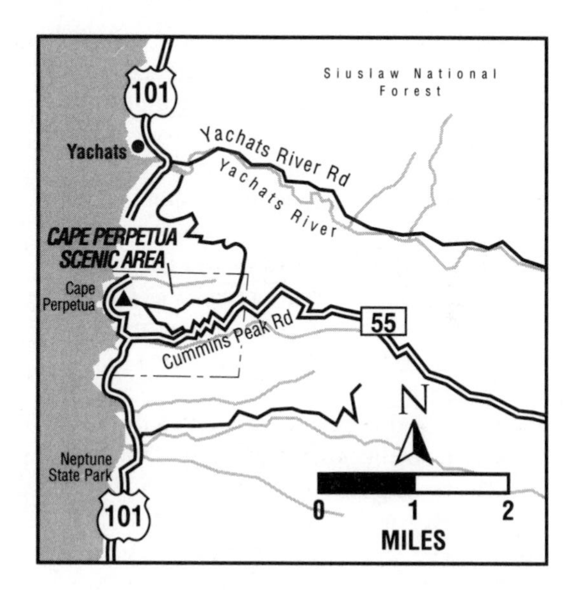

While tourism's growth has been dramatic only recently, all the makings for it were first put in place in the 1930s with the building of this section of U.S.101 along with the construction of the first Cape Perpetua Visitor Center by the Civilian Conservation Corps. Today's center is a renovated version of the original, and there is still evidence of the Depression-era workers' housing on the trail between the center and the beach.

The center is a good starting point for taking in the sights around this unique place. As the focal point of the surrounding piece of land known as the Cape Perpetua Scenic Area, the center offers educational exhibits and films as well as a small bookshop. Trails from the center lead off into stands of old-growth spruce in one direction and under the highway to the beach in another. All in all, there are 22 miles of hiking trails within the Scenic Area. Flanked by state parks on its north and south sides and a wilderness on the east, the highly photogenic Heceta Head Lighthouse not far south, and the famed Stellar Sea Lion Caves just beyond that, the Scenic Area has no lack of interesting day trips from a base camp at the campground.

Ah, yes. The campground. The Cape Perpetua Campground is actually two campgrounds managed by the Forest Service (as is the rest of the Scenic Area). Both are quite close to the Visitor Center, and the only difference between them is that one is an individual-site complex and the other accommodates groups of up to 50 people. Privacy is not great—mostly provided by Sitka spruce with little ground cover. On the other hand, the ocean breezes blow right through and keep insects to a minimum.

Both campgrounds operate mid-May to late September, but it's worth mentioning that the wild and windswept Cape Perpetua is an enormously popular whale-watching spot in the wintertime. Although the campgrounds are not open, the visitor center has interpretive programs for the whale-watching crowd.

If you want to witness prime examples of the geologic magnificence of the Cape Perpetua Scenic Area close up, stop at Devil's Churn and Captain Cook's Chasm. The relentless movement of sea against basalt has formed overhanging cliffs and caves that are pounded even more mercilessly at high tides by clashing currents that explode as high as 60 feet into the air. The effect is exhilarating.

All along this portion of the sculpted coast is an endless array of rugged inlets, crescent-shaped coves, and towering capes. Just south of Devil's Churn is the road up to the Cape Perpetua Viewpoint. At 800 feet above the sea, you can have a bird's-eye look in all directions over this breathtaking panorama.

To get there from Yachats (23 miles south of Newport), drive 3 miles south on U.S. 101. The park entrance is on the non-ocean side.

KEY INFORMATION

Cape Perpetua Scenic Area
P.O. Box 274
Yachats, OR 97498

Operated by: Siuslaw National Forest

Information: (541) 563-3211

Open: Mid-May to late September

Individual sites: 37

Each site has: Picnic tables, fire grill

Site assignment: Reservations and advance deposit required for group camp; otherwise first come, first served

Registration: Self-registration on site

Facilities: Flush toilets, piped water, sanitation station, group camp, public telephone at visitor center

Parking: At campsite

Fee: $10 per night

Elevation: Just above sea level

Restrictions:

Pets–On leash

Fires–In fire pits only

Alcoholic beverages–Permitted

Vehicles–RVs up to 22 feet

EAGLE CREEK CAMPGROUND

Bonneville, Oregon

Yes, the Columbia River Gorge does have a campground that is not overrun with tourists in RVs. Try Eagle Creek Campground between the towns of Bonneville and Cascade Locks in the Columbia River Gorge National Scenic and Recreation Area.

This decent-sized campground is run by the Columbia Gorge Ranger District of the Mount Hood National Forest, sitting just east of the Bonneville Dam. The campground can be easily missed by many Columbia Gorge travelers whose eyes are directed riverward to the massive piece of concrete that provides hydroelectric power to the metropolitan areas farther west.

Despite its proximity to this hulking tribute to human engineering, Eagle Creek offers a woodsy setting amidst true fir, western red cedar and hemlock, and access to some beautiful walks high above the river in the Columbia Wilderness. The busy freeway teeming with tourists and tractor-trailer combinations quickly fades into oblivion as Eagle Creek Trail leaves the end of Forest Service Road 241 beside the campground and follows Eagle Creek for 13 miles to Wahtum Lake and the intersection with Pacific Crest National Scenic Trail.

Along the way the trail passes high cliffs along Eagle Creek and waterfalls too numerous to mention, then crests atop a broad plateau that looks out

CAMPGROUND RATINGS

Beauty:	★★★★
Site privacy:	★★★★
Site spaciousness:	★★★
Quiet:	★★★ (summer)
	★★★★★ (off-season)
Security:	★★★
Cleanliness/upkeep:	★★★★
Insect control:	★★★

If you're cruising along I-84 into Portland along the Columbia River and you've just about given up hope of finding a campground that is not a sea of RVs, all is not lost.

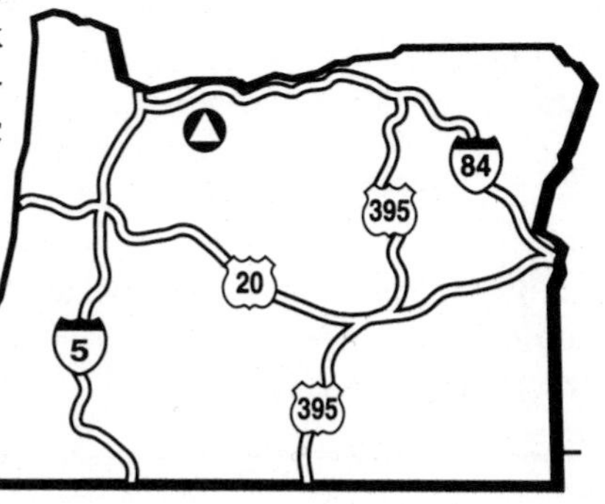

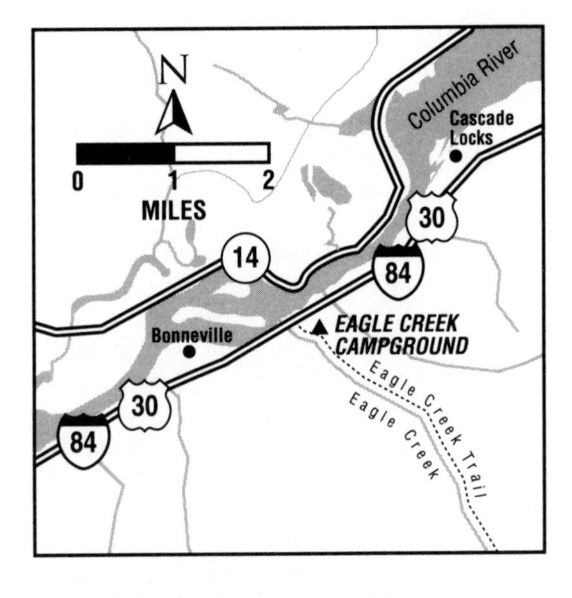

over the expansive Columbia River Gorge and south to Mount Hood. The abundance of waterfalls is your clue to the rapidly dropping (or steepening as you head inland) terrain and should suggest that the climb up to Waucoma Ridge is a healthy one. If you have any doubts, consider that the elevation gain is more than 3,500 feet from trailhead to Wahtum Lake.

Several other trails and Forest Service roads lead off very near the campground to other points within the Columbia Wilderness. A loop trip is possible by following Ruckel Creek Trail 405, then 405B to the Pacific Crest Trail, and turning back toward the Columbia on the Pacific Crest Trail. Trail 400 connects with the Pacific Crest Trail and parallels I-84 back to camp. This loop is roughly equivalent to the one-way distance up to Wahtum but with enough elevation gain to get the heart pumping and the legs straining. For the most accurate picture of the 125 miles of trails within the Columbia Wilderness, check with the Forest Service at its district headquarters in Troutdale.

Weatherwise, this is an area of transition that begins the hand-off from moisture-laden western Oregon to the more arid climes in the east. The Gorge itself adds its own wind-tunnel effect, so be prepared for variety even in summer. Thunderstorms materialize quickly, and the wind can blow hard, particularly in late afternoon. In fact, the Columbia River has an international reputation among sailboarders for this exact reason. Hood River, about 20 miles east of Eagle Creek and once a quiet farming and fishing community, has become a mecca of sailboard mania, with renovated hotels, bed-and-breakfast inns, trendy shops, espresso bars, and cafes catering to the transient population that literally comes and goes with the wind.

Long before there were giant monstrosities like dams on the Columbia, Native Americans were the first to experience the winds of the Columbia. Lewis and Clark were the first white explorers to use the river as a highway, opening the door to continued use by settlers who, at The Dalles, traded Conestoga wagons for the steamboats that carried them to their new homes in the Northwest territory. Rapids and falls that had to be portaged then no longer exist today because the wild and mighty flow of the Columbia has been harnessed by power companies in this century.

For those curious and wanting a respite from outdoor activities, the Bonneville Dam gives tours daily. Other points of interest nearby—both indoors and out—include Cascade Locks, Crown Point Vista House and Observatory, Multnomah Falls and Multnomah Falls Lodge, Bridal Veil Falls, and Fort Dalles Museum.

To get there from Portland, drive 33 miles east on I-84 to the campground. It's 2 miles past the town of Bonneville just off the interstate.

KEY INFORMATION

Eagle Creek Campground
c/o Columbia Gorge Ranger District
31520 SE Woodard Road
Troutdale, OR 97060

Operated by: Mount Hood National Forest

Information: (541) 386-2333

Open: Mid-May to October

Individual sites: 17

Each site has: Picnic table, fire pit with grill

Site assignment: First come, first served; by reservation for groups

Registration: Self-registration on site

Facilities: Bathhouse with toilets and piped water; boat launch nearby

Parking: At individual sites

Fee: $8 per night

Elevation: Sea level

Restrictions:

Pets–On leash

Fires–In fire pits only

Alcoholic beverages–Permitted

Vehicles–RVs and trailers up to 22 feet

EEL CREEK CAMPGROUND

Winchester Bay, Oregon

Welcome to the heart of Oregon Dunes National Recreation Area. If you've never ventured into this stunning sector of the Oregon coast, prepare yourself for an experience that you will not forget.

Eel Creek is just one of many campgrounds that are clustered in the Florence/Reedsport/Coos Bay stretch of U.S. 101. Aside from its vegetation-lush private sites, Eel Creek's strongest selling point is the absence of off-road vehicle access to the dunes.

Why these noisy machines are allowed in a place of such serene and fragile beauty is beyond me. Fortunately there are 32,000 acres of sand in Dungeness National Recreation Area, and the jeep trail stops short a mile or two south of Eel Creek, so there's space for everyone here. If you want peace and quiet as part of your dunes experience, make sure you're not hiking in an area where they rent dune buggies.

Eel Creek backs up against some of the largest dunes in the 46-mile-long protected beach. Always shifting, always changing, there are dunes that reach as high as 600 feet. Slog your way to the top of one of these monsters and look out over a most spectacular sight—sand, sand, and more sand. Swirled and sculpted in some places, smoothed and glistening like satin in others, rising and falling like patterns of the sea frozen in motion, the pale undulations radiate under a startlingly blue August sky.

CAMPGROUND RATINGS

Beauty:	★★★★★
Site privacy:	★★★★★
Site spaciousness:	★★★★
Quiet:	★★★★★
Security:	★★★★
Cleanliness/upkeep:	★★★★
Insect control:	★★★

Backed against some of the largest dunes in Oregon Dunes National Recreation Area, Eel Creek affords a stunning and unforgettable outdoor experience.

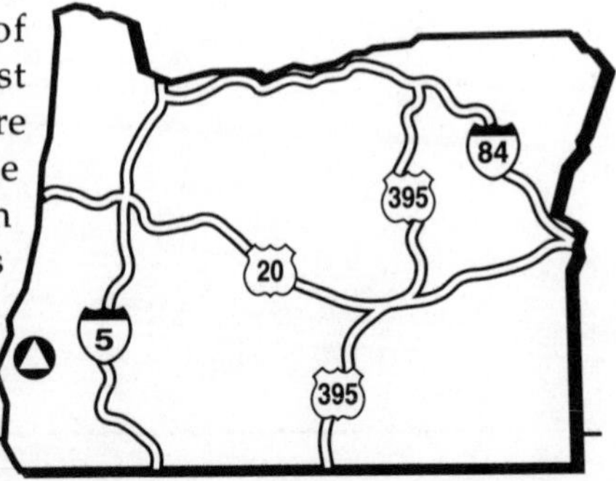

The Pacific Ocean is solely responsible for these magnificent mounds, starting some 13,000 years ago when glacial sediment first began the tireless task of forming this section of Oregon's coast. Since then, rivers out of the nearby Coast Ranges have also contributed their share of deposits. Seasonal patterns of wind and waves combine to add their influence to the sand's destiny, making these the largest collection of active or "living" coastal sand dunes in America.

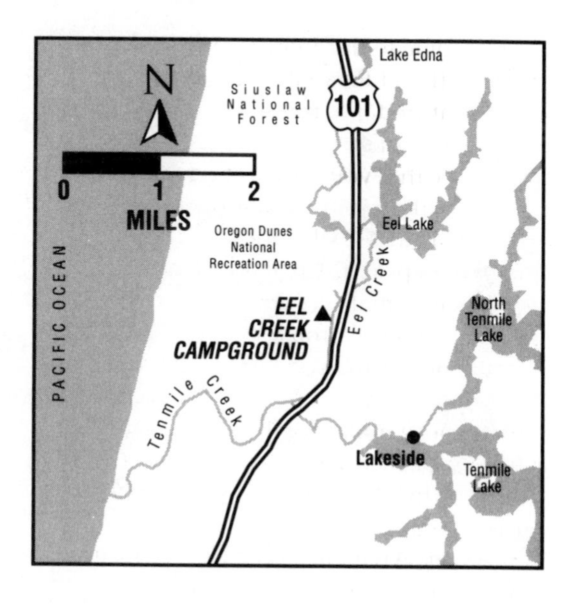

Believe it or not, from Eel Creek Campground due west to the ocean is roughly 2 miles. There are places in Dungeness National Recreation Area where the dunes are as much as 3 miles wide—a stiff distance when you're making your way through soft sand. The easiest traverse is along any of the 30 hiking trails within the Recreation Area. It is best to keep to the trails for more noble reasons as well. This is a highly fragile ecosystem with more than 400 different wildlife species inhabiting the dunes. Of these, 175 are birds.

Headquarters for Oregon Dunes National Recreation Area is right on U.S. 101 at the junction of State Route 38 in Reedsport. This is a well-stocked information bureau with plenty of free guides, brochures, maps, and assorted publications. The exhibits are worth a look, too. It's also a place to compare notes with other travelers.

As with many other parts of western Oregon, late summer and early fall are prime times weatherwise to enjoy the dunes at their best. If it's any indication of winter conditions, Reedsport holds an annual Storm festival in February. Wind speeds have been clocked as high as 100 miles an hour. Generally it's the wind that's more problematic than the wet. Even in summer, clear skies and warm temperatures are tempered by the incessant offshore breezes that often kick up little flurries of sand that playfully tickle the ankles but can be aggravating at eye level. Sand inside a camera body can be ruinous (a.k.a., costly), so protect your equipment.

Aside from the mesmerizing appeal of the dunes, you'll find a variety of other attractions. The Winchester Bay area offers guided and chartered fishing options, clamming spots too numerous to mention, and a museum and lighthouse. Inland along the Umpqua River is Dean Creek Elk Viewing Area, a 923-acre preserve for free-roaming Roosevelt elk which are native to the area. The spot also attracts a multitude of waterfowl and migratory birds as well as osprey, bald eagles, and blue herons. Most of Eel Creek Campground is open only June to late September, but recently the decision was made to keep one loop of the campground open all year. Take advantage of this and go when the crowds of summer disperse.

It's easy to confuse this campground with Mid Eel, which is only minutes away. Watch for signs to Eel Creek Campground about 12 miles south of Reedsport. The campground is right off U.S. 101 but surprisingly quiet for such close proximity to a busy thoroughfare. Heavy vegetation helps absorb traffic sounds and provides lovely secluded, sandy-bottomed tent sites. Ocean breezes help keep insects to a minimum.

To get there from Reedsport, drive south on US 101 for 12 miles. The campground entrance is on the ocean side.

KEY INFORMATION

Eel Creek Campground
Oregon Dunes National Recreation Area
855 Highway Avenue
Reedsport, OR 97467

Operated by: Siuslaw National Forest, Oregon Dunes National Recreation Area

Information: (541) 271-3611

Open: 1 loop open all year; rest of campground open May to late September

Individual sites: 51

Each site has: Picnic table, fire grill

Site assignment: First come, first served; no reservations

Registration: Self-registration or camp host collects

Facilities: Bathhouse with flush toilets and hot water; boat launch and rentals nearby; Friday night interpretive program

Parking: At individual sites

Fee: $10 per night, $8 each additional vehicle

Elevation: Sea level

Restrictions:

Pets–On leash

Fires–In fire pits only

Alcoholic beverages–Permitted

Vehicles–RVs and trailers up to 22 feet

ELK LAKE CAMPGROUND

Detroit, Oregon

The word "foolhardy" may come to mind as you find yourself at the junction that leads to this gem of a spot in Willamette National Forest, about 10 miles above the small, historic burg of Detroit.

"Rough Road" is the more-than-understated message on the sign that the Forest Service has (jokingly?) placed at the intersection of FS 4696 and FS 4697. I can only interpret this gesture as the agency's attempt at a little black wilderness humor. The road is decidedly rough but, we found, not impassable. As long as your exhaust system and oil pan sit high and secure, you should be okay.

Hugging the southern boundary of Bull of the Woods Wilderness, peaceful Elk Lake is aptly named for the huge herds of elk that used to graze in this area. It lies in the subalpine laps of Battle Ax Mountain, Mount Beachie, and Gold Butte and is a classic Cascade escape that probably remains so because the Forest Service insists on not improving the road into it. (On the other hand, it may be a matter of funds.) Elk Lake Campground sits at the western tip of this peanut-shaped lake and is accessible by following the road along the north side of the lake to the short spur that drops down off the main road to the left.

CAMPGROUND RATINGS

Beauty:	★★★★★
Site privacy:	★★★★
Site spaciousness:	★★★★★
Quiet:	★★★★★
Security:	★★★
Cleanliness/upkeep:	★★★★
Insect control:	★★★

Beware: The road in is rough with a capital R. But once there, you'll find this is a great base camp for exploring Willamette National Forest.

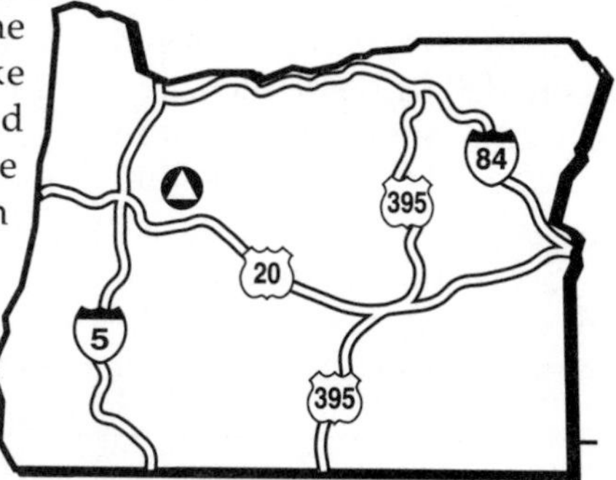

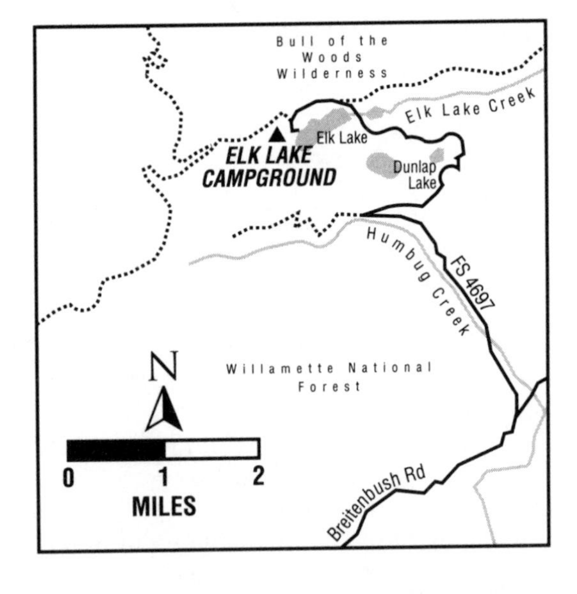

Elk Lake's campsites are strung along the shore of the lake. Tall stands of Douglas fir and western hemlock share the land with white fir, birches, Oregon grape, ferns, and trillium to offer a prime collection of natural cover. In early July, pink-blossomed rhododendrons seem somehow out of place in this rugged, woodsy setting.

This campground may be tough to get to, but once you're there, it makes for a terrific base camp while you enjoy the recreational options. At the top of the list is hiking into Bull of the Woods Wilderness, which is home to one of western Oregon's few remaining old-growth forests. From Beachie Saddle (about a mile west of the campground on FS 4697), trailheads strike out for Battle Ax Mountain to the north (into the wilderness), Mount Beachie to the south. This section of FS 4697 is not recommended for any motor vehicles; consider this a warm-up for the steep 2-mile and 1.5-mile (respectively) grunts up these peaks to views that are well worth the effort. A less strenuous hike follows Elk Lake Creek northeast into Bull of the Woods Wilderness from a trailhead near where the creek feeds its namesake. For extended trips into the wilderness backcountry, take the trail that leaves very near the campground spur road.

I should mention that Bull of the Woods Wilderness is a non-permit area as of this writing, but you may want to check the current status.

If you are thinking Elk Lake might be a nice spot to take in lazy kayaking or canoeing, you're right. Anyone foolhardy enough to drag a boat into this remote locale deserves to be rewarded (or psychoanalyzed). An undeveloped put-in accommodates inflatable rafts, kayaks, canoes, and other small, nonmotorized craft. Pick up a fishing permit at the general store in Detroit if you have thoughts of angling for your dinner. For either boating or fishing, don't overlook little Dunlap Lake (named for an early-day prospector) that is hidden from view about a mile before you get to Elk Lake. Forest Service road exploration also awaits if you had the foresight to bring your mountain bike along. Test your skill back down the 2-mile "riverbed" and pedal on up FS 4696 (to the left) to Gold Butte. The views of mountain peaks from this formerly manned fire lookout are staggering on a clear day—north to Mount Hood, east to Mount Jefferson, south to Mount Washington. Farther up FS 46 is Breitenbush Hot Springs, worth a dip for tired muscles.

To get there from Detroit (50 miles southeast of Salem), drive north on FS 46 (Breitenbush Road) for 4.5 miles to FS 4697. Follow this for 10 miles to the campground. Stay to the left fork where FS 4697 and FS 4696 intersect at about 8 miles. The last 2 miles are extremely rough.

KEY INFORMATION

Elk Lake Campground
c/o Detroit Ranger District
HC 73, Box 320
Mill City, OR 97360

Operated by: Willamette National Forest

Information: (503) 854-3366

Open: July to late September

Individual sites: 14

Some sites have: Picnic table, fire pit with grill, shade trees

Site assignment: First come, first served; no reservations

Registration: Not necessary

Facilities: Pit toilets, no piped water; primitive boat launch; no garbage service, pack out all garbage

Parking: At individual sites and in general parking area (short walk to some campsites); 4 x 4 recommended

Fee: No fee

Elevation: 4,000 feet

Restrictions:

Pets–On leash

Fires–In fire pits only

Alcoholic beverages–Permitted

Vehicles–Not recommended for low-clearance RVs

Other–Fishing permit required

MARYS PEAK

Philomath, Oregon

On a clear day, the views from atop Marys Peak are unparalleled. Mount Rainier is visible to the north, Mount Hood to the east, Mount Jefferson to the south. The Alsea River Valley, favored by fishermen from the Corvallis/Eugene area for its bountiful steelhead, fall chinook, and coho salmon, fans out to the west with the glistening Pacific beyond. The Alsea is just one of a dozen major rivers sliding out of the Coast Ranges and into the Pacific.

At 4,097 feet, you are standing on the highest point in the Oregon Coast Ranges. There's something exhilarating about knowing that you are looking down on everything for as far as the eye can see.

If you are not already familiar with the Coast Ranges weather, you won't know that cloudless days on Marys Peak are rare indeed. Siuslaw National Forest, within which Marys Peak is located, is known as a coastal rain forest. That will give you some idea of the degree of wetness that pervades the place. The average rainfall is 90 inches annually in Siuslaw. There are normally as many as 180 days of measurable precipitation.

Driest times are late summer and early fall. Wintertime can actually be quite good when a substantial snowfall covers the peak and makes it an ideal, untracked wonderland for cross-coun-

CAMPGROUND RATINGS

Beauty:	★★★★
Site privacy:	★★★
Site spaciousness:	★★★
Quiet:	★★★★★
Security:	★★★★
Cleanliness/upkeep:	★★★★★
Insect control:	★★

An intimate tents-only site at the highest point in the Oregon Coast Ranges.

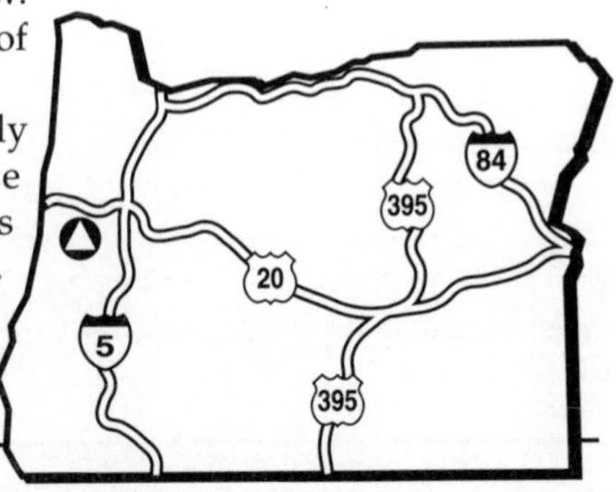

try skiers. The campground is closed but snow-park permits are available from the Forest Service.

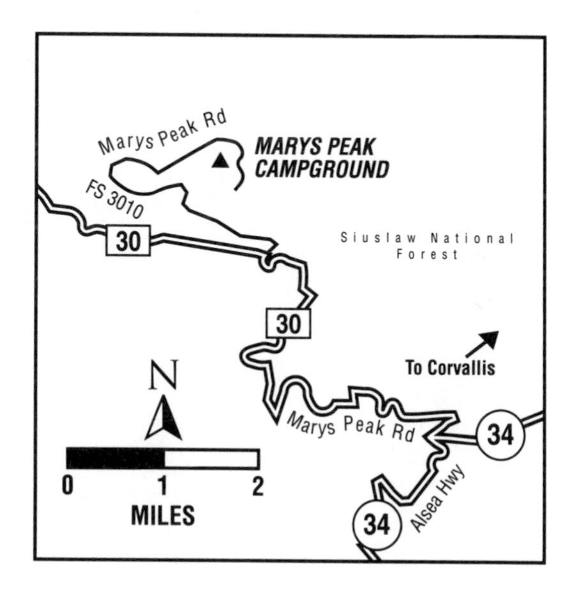

The same meadows that are cross-country routes in winter are flower-filled delights in the spring. Predominant year-round are the everpresent evergreens: Douglas, noble, and Pacific silver fir at the higher elevations, with an understory of sword ferns, salal, and oxalis. Stands of western hemlock grow so thickly at lower elevations that the lack of sunshine keeps the underbrush at a low ebb.

Unfortunately, the Forest Service has allowed disastrous quantities of timber to be cut on Marys Peak in the past, but a renewed effort is underway to attempt to reforest these areas. Marys Peak Scenic Botanical Area is an experiment to preserve the noble fir and to restimulate its growth. This should not only restore the natural beauty of the area, but it will also continue to provide woodland creatures such as deer, grouse, and squirrels with habitat.

Marys Peak (and all of the Coast Ranges for that matter) sits on ancient basalt that was part of the Pacific Ocean floor some 50 to 60 million years ago. Constant uplifting and shifting by tectonic plates keep pushing the mountain range ever upward, although the evidence of this activity is not as easily seen on Marys Peak as it is elsewhere in the range. The dense forest and thick mulchy soil obscure geologic evidence, making this one of the toughest areas for geologists to examine accurately.

Sidetrips in the Marys Peak vicinity include the South Fork Alsea River Byway, the Benton County Scenic Loop, William L. Finley National Wildlife Refuge, the Willamette Floodplain, Benton County Historical Museum in Philomath, Corvallis Arts Center, and Horner Museum, also in Corvallis. There's a nice bike path between Corvallis and Philomath that follows the Willamette and Marys Rivers. Mountain biking on the zillion Forest Service roads in Siuslaw National Forest requires a very good map.

To get there from Philomath (6 miles southwest of Corvallis), follow Alsea Highway (SR 34) southwest for roughly 10 miles to Marys Peak Road (FS 30) and turn right. Follow Marys Peak Road, which becomes FS 3010, to its end and the campground.

KEY INFORMATION

Marys Peak Campground
c/o Alsea Ranger District
Alsea, OR 97324

Operated by: Siuslaw National Forest

Information: (541) 487-5811

Open: May 1 to October 31

Individual sites: 6

Each site has: Picnic table, fire pit, shade trees

Site assignment: First come, first served; no reservations

Registration: Self-registration on site

Facilities: Bathhouse with toilets, sinks, running water

Parzking: At individual sites

Fee: $5 per night, $2 each additional vehicle

Elevation: 3,800 feet

Restrictions:

Pets–On leash

Fires–In fire pits only

Alcoholic beverages–Permitted

Vehicles–No RVs or trailers

NATURAL BRIDGE CAMPGROUND

Prospect, Oregon

Often overlooked by travelers scurrying between the heavily promoted majesty of Crater Lake and the famed Wild and Scenic sections of the lower Rogue River, the upper Rogue River area offers its own style of spectacular scenery and wilderness treasures that should satisfy the desires of most outdoor adventurers. If you're set on experiencing the beauty of the Rogue by boat, however, you'll be disappointed to discover that this section of the river is off limits to kayaks and canoes. Head on down to Grants Pass or the town of Rogue River, and they'll take care of you there.

Here, in upper Rogue River territory, the river plummets out of its source in Crater Lake National Park at a rate of as much as 48 feet per mile. Take a look down from precipitous heights along State Route 62 north of Natural Bridge Campground for perhaps the clearest indication of why this portion of the river is so unrunnable. A flash of silver far below is the Rogue hurling itself seaward through the deep, narrow fissure known as the Rogue River Gorge.

Natural Bridge is so named for the unique feature adjacent to it. It is at this point that the upper Rogue disappears from sight and runs underground for 200 feet. The campground sits virtually on top of water flowing beneath it.

CAMPGROUND RATINGS

Beauty:	★★★★★
Site privacy:	★★★★★
Site spaciousness:	★★★
Quiet:	★★★★
Security:	★★★★
Cleanliness/upkeep:	★★★★★
Insect control:	★★★★

A good place to set up camp and explore the beautiful often-overlooked upper Rogue River area. Be sure to take a map!

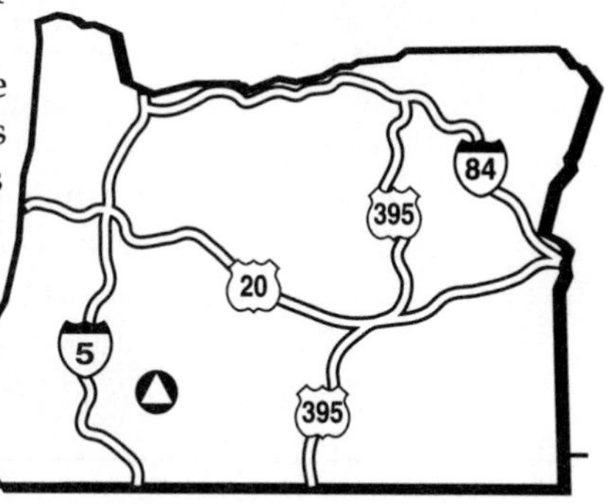

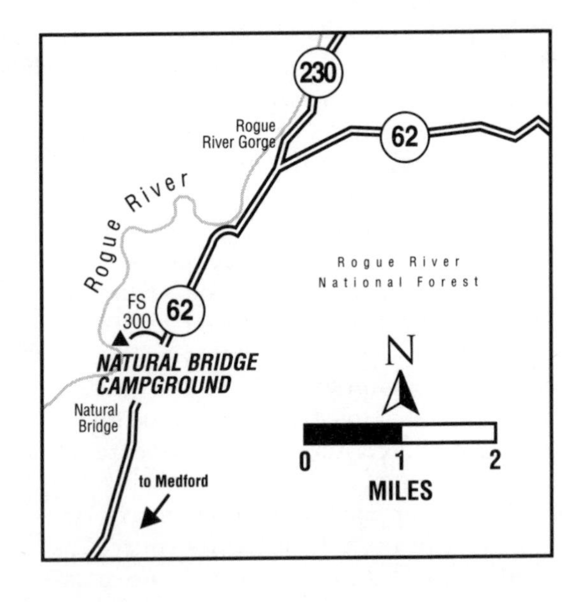

Natural Bridge is one of several campgrounds in the vicinity that is located on the banks of the Rogue or on small creeks that feed it. Given its proximity to Crater Lake, this area can be quite busy in the summertime, but the larger, more developed campsites tend to fill up first. The lack of piped water at Natural Bridge discourages those who are not prepared for primitive conditions. The surrounding Rogue River National Forest is characterized by dense forests of Douglas fir and sugar pine that soften the contours of a high plateau upon which the forests grow. Over 450 miles of trails within the national forest lead to remote high country lakes, ridgetop vistas, and the seclusion of Rogue-Umpqua Divide Wilderness. Some of the routes connect with trails into the adjoining Umpqua National Forest.

Numerous day hikes and extended backpacking trips will reveal not only the natural splendor of this undisturbed country but also the diverse wildlife and plant species that thrive in the moderate climate. The most famous inhabitant in the upper Rogue country is the northern spotted owl, who shares his home in this lush expanse with an astonishing assortment of nocturnal creatures.

Except for the highest altitudes, which receive sizable measures of snow in the winter, the area enjoys warm and dry summers, with most of the 20 to 40 inches of annual precipitation occurring between October and May.

This rugged land is full of thick vegetation. Getting lost can happen easily. Make sure you have a good topographic or Forest Service map with you when you head out for lonely and distant spots. Booklets of maps and trail guides are available at Rogue River National Forest headquarters in Medford or at the district office in Prospect.

If you are looking for an ambitious overland trek, consider Upper Rogue River Trail, which follows the river along its banks for many miles until it intersects with Pacific Crest National Scenic Trail in Crater Lake National Park. The Upper Rogue Trail is known by few and used by even fewer, affording an intimate experience with an untrammeled part of the famous Rogue. For an even more unusual treat, try a bit of Nordic skiing along sections of the trail in winter. Climbers with level 1-4 skills may want to test their ability on an odd geologic formation near the Rogue-Umpqua Divide Wilderness boundary. A pair of 400-foot spires known as Rabbit Ears was first climbed in 1921 and continues to intrigue the adventuresome.

To get there, travel northeast on SR 62 (Crater Lake Highway) about 32 miles from Medford. From the Prospect turnoff, continue north on SR 62 another 12 miles or so to FS 300. Turn left, and the campground is 1 mile in.

From Crater Lake, take SR 62 west if you are leaving the park from the south. If you exit from the north side, follow SR 138 to its intersection with SR 230. Head west and eventually south on SR 230 until it becomes SR 62. You'll turn right onto FS 300 about 3 miles from this point.

KEY INFORMATION

Natural Bridge Campground
c/o Prospect Ranger District
Prospect, OR 97536

Operated by: Rogue River National Forest

Information: (541) 560-3623 May to early November

Open: Late May to early November

Individual sites: 16

Each site has: Picnic table, fire pit with grill, shade trees

Site assignment: First come, first served; no reservations

Registration: Not necessary

Facilities: Vault toilets, no piped water

Parking: At individual sites

Fee: No fee

Elevation: 3,300 feet

Restrictions:

Pets–On leash

Fires–In fire pits only

Alcoholic beverages–Permitted

Vehicles–RVs and trailers up to 22 feet

OSWALD WEST STATE PARK

Nehalem, Oregon

In the tradition of the beautiful state park system that makes Oregon camping such a pleasurable experience, Oswald West is a crown jewel.

It is a rather unique crown jewel, actually. There are 36 primitive walk-in tent sites that are reached by a one-third-mile trail from the parking area. The park service provides wheelbarrows for carting your camp gear up and down the angled, paved pathway. Part of the camaraderie that quickly accompanies a camping trip to Oswald comes from the exchanges of greetings, sympathy, and an occasional helping hand that fellow campers offer as they push, pull, tug, and otherwise maneuver their overloaded carts between car and campsite. It is not unusual to find a heap of spilled goods lying in the path as a frustrated youngster valiantly attempts to right his overturned one-wheeled craft before Dad comes looking to see what in the world is taking so darned long.

It's all in the spirit of camping at Oswald West, but you can tell the veterans from the novices around here. They've learned to travel light.

The lush surroundings are the first thing you'll probably notice when you descend into the inner sanctum of this primeval coastal rain forest. The trees here look as old as time, soaring skyward and looking formidable in their heavy, shaggy

CAMPGROUND RATINGS

Beauty:	★★★★★
Site privacy:	★★★★
Site spaciousness:	★★★★
Quiet:	★★★★
Security:	★★★
Cleanliness/upkeep:	★★★★
Insect control:	★

One of Oregon's best state park campgrounds. Primitive walk-in sites in an inner sanctum of coastal rain forest.

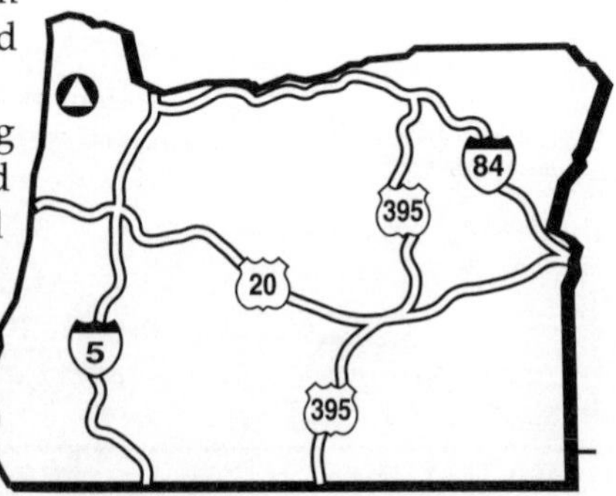

coats of moss. The campsites are private little grottos of greenery interspersed among the venerable collection of western red cedar, hemlock, and Sitka spruce. The entire camping grounds are shrouded in a rich undercover of salal, sword ferns, huckleberry and salmonberry bushes, with wildflowers such as trillium and skunk cabbage adding spots of color when in bloom.

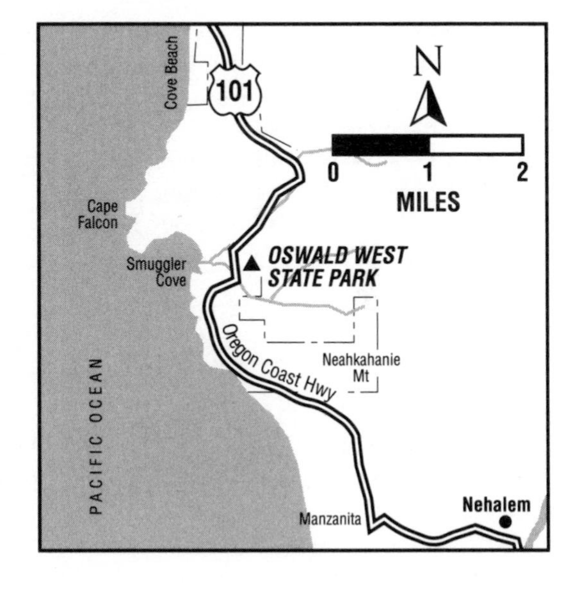

Getting around the campground is easiest by way of established trails. Crashing through the underbrush to use the restroom is a definite camping faux pas. It is a rare treat to have flush toilets in such an undeveloped facility.

The Coast Ranges hug the Pacific along this section of the Oregon coast, resulting in steep bluffs that rise high above the shoreline but limit the beachcombing options. Short Sands Beach, within the protective curve of Smuggler's Cove, is the only choice in an expanse of 2,500 acres of parkland that stretches from Arch Cape to Neahkahnie Beach. It's a good spot to watch surfers ride the waves as they thread their way through tricky waters dotted with rock "stacks."

Headlands hiking is an alternative activity. Both Cape Falcon and Neahkahanie Mountain have trails to the top for dramatic views. The 3-mile route up Neahkahanie zigzags its way to a 1,710-foot promontory, with views north that extend beyond the Columbia River. In all, there are 15 miles of trails in "Os West," as it is affectionately known by the locals. Twelve of these are part of the lengthy Oregon Coast Trail. Ask the park rangers for more information about this popular and unique trail.

Rain forest conditions mean wet weather regularly as the moisture-heavy marine clouds meet the unyielding Coast Ranges and dump their load on Oswald West. It can also be quite blustery. An extreme example came in 1982 when gales raging at more than 150 miles per hour leveled six million board feet of old-growth Sitka spruce on Cape Falcon. It took two years to replant the area, and the loss of those huge, old conifers will never be fully compensated.

The park's peak season is June through August, but some of the best weather occurs in September and October. In spring, Neahkahanie Mountain provides a splendid display of wildflowers in bloom, particularly the pink coast fawn lily.

To get there from Cannon Beach, drive south on U.S. 101 for about 10 miles. Access to the campground is from the southernmost parking lot, which may be full. Overflow parking areas are nearby.

KEY INFORMATION

Oswald West State Park
8300R Third Street Necarney
Nehalem, OR 97131

Operated by: Oregon State Parks and Recreation

Information: (503) 368-5943

Open: March through October

Individual sites: 36 primitive, walk-in

Each site has: Picnic table, fire pit, piped water, shade trees

Site assignment: First come, first served; no reservations

Registration: Self-registration on site

Facilities: Bathhouse with toilets, sinks, running water; wheelbarrows for transporting gear; firewood

Parking: In-campground parking lot at trailhead

Fee: $14 per night

Elevation: Sea level

Restrictions:

Pets–On leash

Fires–In fire pits only

Alcoholic beverages–Permitted

Vehicles–No RV or trailer accommodations; no bicycles on park trails

OXBOW PARK

Gresham, Oregon

As one of the nation's leading conservation-minded states, Oregon's Oxbow Park sets a prime example of what a metropolitan park can and should be. The grounds are a sprawling 1,000 acres of dense forests, grassy clearings, sandy river frontage, and sheer canyon walls. Old-growth forest alone covers 180 acres. Native salmon spawn within one-fourth-mile of camping areas on Sandy River, known as the top-rated winter steelhead stream in Oregon. Wildlife abounds in the park, with more than 200 native plant varieties, 100 bird species, nearly 40 different mammals, and an interesting assortment of reptiles and water-dwelling creatures. The park employs a full-time naturalist year-round, who is busiest in summer with a heavy schedule of public and private programs.

The first order of business once you get settled into your campsite is to explore the trails on foot. There are roughly 15 miles of trails that follow Sandy River and wind throughout the park. It's easy to lose yourself to the spaciousness and ramble to your heart's content with no more important thought than to see how many of the birds on the park's list (available at the office) you can identify. Wander into the old-growth forest and contemplate a summer idyll. There's a small waterfall nearby to enhance your poetic musings.

CAMPGROUND RATINGS

Beauty:	★★★★★
Site privacy:	★★★★
Site spaciousness:	★★★★
Quiet:	★★★★
Security:	★★★★★
Cleanliness/upkeep:	★★★★
Insect control:	★★★★

Located an easy 20 miles from downtown Portland in the lovely and lush Sandy River Gorge, Oxbow Park is an amazing blend of recreational diversity, scenic delight, and environmental consciousness.

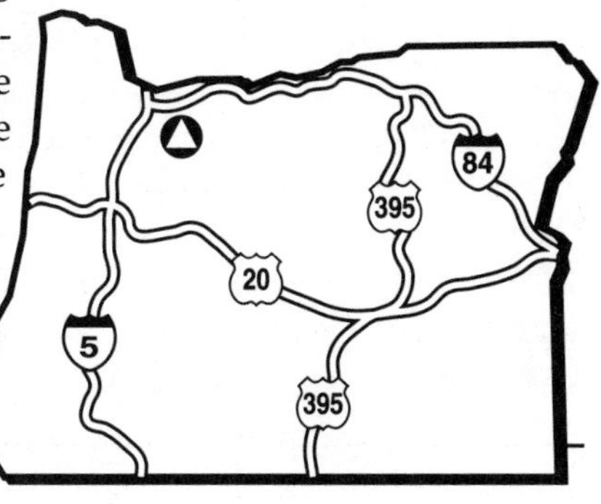

Slip through the underbrush to a sun-warmed curve in the river and wriggle your toes in the sand. Even at the height of the summer season, you'll be amazed at how quickly you can find seclusion.

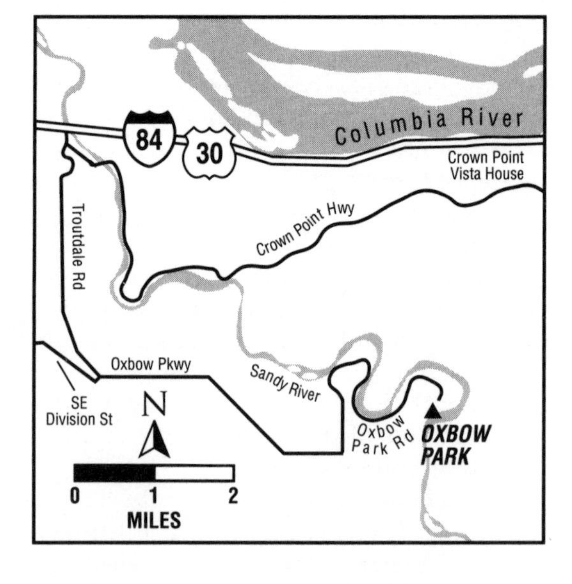

For a different perspective of the trail system, the park allows horses on most of the pathways. There are designated equestrian unloading areas, and trailhead markers indicate those that are restricted.

Fishing and boating activities are undeniably central to the popularity of Oxbow Park and Sandy River. Most often they go hand in hand. There are very few times of the year when anglers won't find a reason to cast their lines into the broad and shallow waters. Along with its preeminent status as a steelheader's delight, the Sandy also sports healthy quantities of coho, fall chinook, spring chinook, and summer steelhead. Check with the park office for fishing regulations on the Sandy as they differ from other Oregon rivers.

Recreational boating on this section of the Sandy is limited to nonmotorized craft, thanks to its recent inclusion under both state and federal Wild and Scenic protection. Above Oxbow Park and dependent on flow levels, there is Class III and IV whitewater for experienced kayakers, rafters, and canoeists to enjoy. A popular run is the 6 miles between Dodge Park and Oxbow, affording exclusive views of this section of the river gorge. Downstream from Oxbow to Lewis and Clark State Park is a pleasant drift trip with gentle ripples and refreshing pools for an occasional dip. Additional river and boat rental information is available at the park office.

If you're interested in exploring beyond the park's boundaries, Oxbow can be the starting point for a couple of scenic drives that take in a lot with minimal time commitments. The shorter of the two is the route along Crown Point Highway, named for the 700-foot piece of basalt that spires above the Columbia River. Crown Point Vista House, with its information center, is well worth the visit, not to mention the staggering views afforded from its lofty perch.

The second route takes you southeast on U.S. 26 through the Sandy River lowlands, around Mount Hood, north to Hood River on SR 35, and back along I-84 to Exit 18 at Lewis and Clark State Park. This is roughly 150 miles of nonstop scenery, with the snowy peak of Mount Hood as the focal point most of the way. From Hood River back to Oxbow, the changing landscape of the Columbia River Gorge unfolds around each bend in the road.

To get there, take the Wood Village Exit 16 off I-84 in Gresham. Go south to Division Street. Turn left, and continue to Oxbow Parkway. From there, follow signs down to the park. The road tends to wind around a bit, and there are several spots where it is easy to make a miscalculated turn. Just keep following the signs. Once you reach the park entrance, it's a sharp and curving drop down into the gorge.

KEY INFORMATION

Oxbow Park
3010 SE Oxbow Parkway
Gresham, OR 97080

Operated by: Multnomah County Parks Service Division

Information: (503) 663-4708

Open: All year; gates close at legal sunset and open at 6:30 a.m.

Individual sites: 45, primarily for tent campers

Each site has: Picnic table, free-standing barbecue pit, shade trees

Some sites have: Piped water

Site assignment: First come, first served; no reservations

Registration: Daily fee collected each evening at campsite; additional one-time fee upon entering park at park entrance

Facilities: Picnic tables, group camps, playground, boat ramp, equestrian area, interpretive programs

Parking: Up to 2 vehicles at campsite

Fee: $9 per night; $2 each additional vehicle; day-use fee: $3 on first day except weekdays, Nov. 1 to May 15, $2 rest of year

Elevation: Sea level

Restrictions:

Pets–Not permitted on park grounds

Fires–In fire pits only; seasonal restrictions depending on dry conditions

Alcoholic beverages–Not permitted

Vehicles–No RV hookups; 12 spaces accommodate trailers up to 35 feet ; no ATVs

Other–No guns or fireworks

SADDLE MOUNTAIN STATE PARK

Cannon Beach, Oregon

Want to enjoy the beach, see the mountains, and not get trampled by the crowds? Saddle Mountain is the answer. Most people hurrying along U.S. 26 between Portland and the ocean beaches in northwestern Oregon pass up this cool, green spot either because they don't know about it or they have an unusual idea of "getting away from it all" in the overdeveloped, overpriced, and overrun (purely my opinion, of course) resorts, motels, inns, rental cottages, RV parks, and various other means of accommodation that are the mainstay of the tourist business in seaside towns from the mouth of the Columbia River to the California border.

Don't get me wrong. I love the Oregon coast. If you want to pay the price, there are scads of wonderful places to stay—by the day, by the week, by the weekend, whatever. And there are still plenty of areas that have been preserved in their natural and undeveloped states that showcase the coastal beauty. But if your interest is tent camping in the purest sense, the Oregon coast may be a disappointment. You'll have to sacrifice ocean proximity for optimum peace and quiet by going farther inland to places such as Saddle Mountain State Park. However, you have the best of both worlds at Saddle Mountain because you'll be less than 15 miles from the nearest coastal attrac-

CAMPGROUND RATINGS

Beauty:	★★
Site privacy:	★★★
Site spaciousness:	★★
Quiet:	★★
Security:	★★
Cleanliness/upkeep:	★
Insect control:	★★★

If the summer crowds on the Oregon coast are more than you can handle but you don't want to forego scenic pleasures entirely, consider Saddle Mountain State Park.

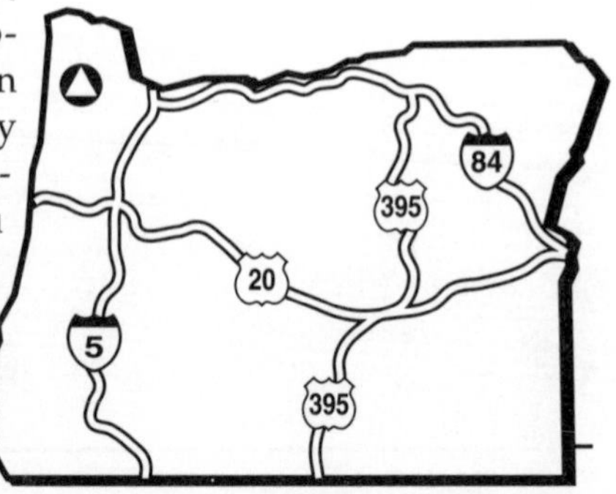

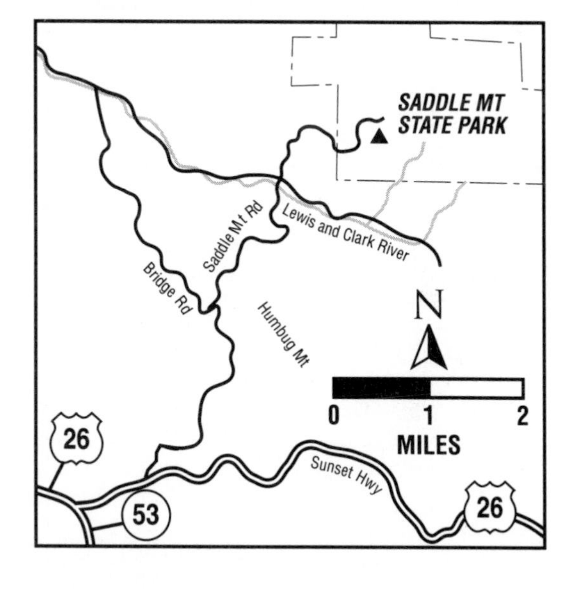

tions of Cannon Beach and Seaside, well away from the crowded Coast Highway corridor, and only a 2.6-mile hike from superb views atop the highest peak in northwestern Oregon. Not a bad combination, really.

Add to that a campground (albeit primitive) that is for tent campers only and nearly 3,000 acres of forests, meadows, and creeks that you'll share with a number of woodland critters and several rare and endangered plant species.

This latter feature will be of particular interest to the weekend botanist. Saddle Mountain was a haven for certain species of plant life during the Ice Age, and much of the flora that has evolved today high on the flanks of this 3,283-foot peak is not found anywhere else. Patterson's bittercress is the most unique, found only on Saddle Mountain and nearby Onion Mountain. The best time to visit Saddle Mountain is early to mid-June, when the alpine wildflowers put on one of the best shows of colors in the region.

For the weekend mountaineer, Saddle Mountain Trail will be a pleasantly surprising challenge with a reward of unending views from the summit. Casual hikers will probably want to stop at the saddle just beyond the fields of flowers. The more adventurous and sure-footed in your party can continue on to the crest, but be forewarned that the path is steep and indistinct in places, making travel, as the park brochure says, "extremely treacherous" and not recommended for those who aren't in the best of shape.

For those who do make it to the top, feast on the views while enjoying that picnic lunch you brought along. To the south is Nehalem Bay and a sprinkle of small characteristic coastal towns. Looking west, the Pacific Ocean paints a blue-green backdrop to the resort towns of Seaside and Cannon Beach, with Tillamook Head and Haystack Rock figuring prominently between them. North is historic Astoria at the intersection of the Columbia River and the Pacific. Fort Clatsop is the site of Lewis and Clark's winter camp in 1805 and 1806. Snowcapped Cascade Mountain peaks to the east add a finishing touch.

The maritime climate of the Pacific can produce some fierce weather. Up to 100 inches of rain annually has been recorded in some areas, so be prepared for wet conditions.

To get there, turn north on Saddle Mountain Road off U.S. 26 about 1.5 miles east of Necanicum Junction. Drive 7 miles to the campground. A picnic area, parking lot (self-contained RVs can park here), and trailhead are all here as well.

KEY INFORMATION

Saddle Mountain State Park
P.O. Box 681
Cannon Beach, OR 97110

Operated by: Oregon State Parks and Recreation

Information: (541) 861-1671

Open: April through October, depending on snow

Individual sites: 10

Each site has: Picnic table, fire pit, piped water, shade trees

Site assignment: First come, first served; no reservations

Registration: Self-registration on site

Facilities: Restrooms with toilets, sinks, running water; firewood

Parking: In campground

Fee: $10 per night

Elevation: 1,900 feet

Restrictions:

Pets–On leash

Fires–In fire pits only

Alcoholic beverages–Permitted

Vehicles–No accommodations for RVs or trailers; self-contained units may use parking lot

THIELSEN VIEW CAMPGROUND

Diamond Lake, Oregon

With two other campgrounds across scenic Diamond Lake that can accommodate several hundred campers between them, chances are you won't find yourself alone out in what will seem like very remote territory.

Diamond Lake is an immensely popular area, particularly for trout fishermen who troll the lake's crystalline waters. The lake's name comes from the abundance of glassy volcanic rock that litters this region of Umpqua National Forest.

Great fishing notwithstanding, Diamond Lake's popularity can be attributed to a number of other factors. For starters, Diamond Lake is one of the largest natural lakes in Oregon. Add to this its proximity to some spectacular mountain scenery. Follow this up with blissfully warm, dry summer weather. Last but not least, the place is a convenient distance from Crater Lake National Park not far to the south (where frightening numbers of visitors gather in any given summer) and quickly absorbs the overflow.

The Diamond Lake area is one of those fantastic natural playgrounds that can turn the most resolute vacation planner into a miserable heap of indecision. So many wonderful places. So little time.

A sizable portion of the wonderfulness around Diamond Lake is in the form of snowy, knife-like mountain peaks—Mount Bailey to the west and, as the

CAMPGROUND RATINGS

Beauty:	★★★★★
Site privacy:	★★★★
Site spaciousness:	★★★★★
Quiet:	★★★★★
Security:	★★★★
Cleanliness/upkeep:	★★★★★
Insect control:	★★★

Thielsen View is one of several Forest Service camps in the Diamond Lake vicinity, but it's somewhat removed from the mayhem of State Route 138 because it sits alone on the western shore.

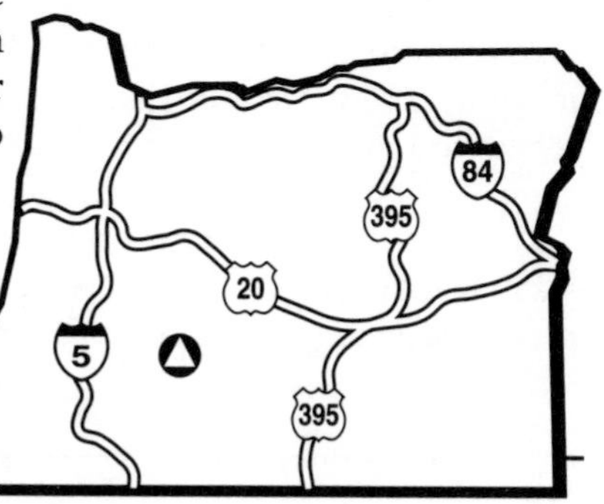

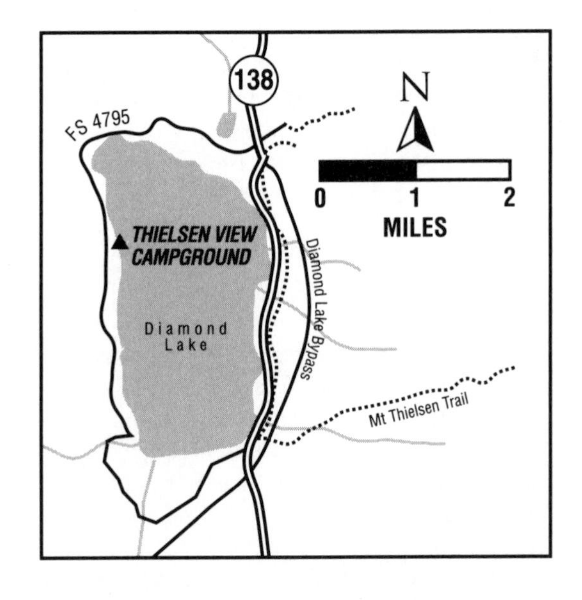

campground name implies, Mount Thielsen to the east. Both will take some time to explore since the only way to fully appreciate them is by foot over arduous trails full of loose, crumbling pumice. The rock is modern-day evidence of the eruption of Mount Mazama some 6,700 years ago.

The upper portion of 9,182-foot Mount Thielsen is a technical climb and should be attempted only by those with the appropriate skills and equipment. Less difficult hikes abound, however, throughout the national forest, Mount Thielsen Wilderness, and Oregon Cascades Recreation Area, all within access of Thielsen View Campground. Mount Thielsen Wilderness alone has roughly 125 miles of hiking trails, including a section of the Pacific Crest National Scenic Trail.

Hiking, however, doesn't become an option at the higher elevations much before June, when the heavy snowfalls of winter melt from the trails. In the meantime and at various times throughout the year, there's mountain biking along Forest Service roads and designated trails (except in wilderness areas), lake and creek fishing, hunting, birdwatching, cross-country skiing, snowmobiling, canoeing and kayaking the North Umpqua River, and lowland walks to Lemolo Falls and Toketee Falls. If nothing else, there's sitting in camp and enjoying incredibly clear mountain air.

Thielsen View Campground sits on the western shore of Diamond Lake at 5,200 feet elevation. The drive from Roseburg off I-5 follows the pristine and picturesque North Umpqua River most of the way on State Route 138. This stretch of highway has been called one of the prettiest drives in western America in the summertime.

To get there from Roseburg and I-5, take SR 138 east/southeast to Clearwater (about 50 miles). At Clearwater, the road leaves the North Umpqua and parallels Clearwater River. At the intersection with FS 4795, turn right and head around the north end of Diamond Lake to find Thielsen View Campground.

From Medford, take U.S. 62 north to SR 230 north, to SR 138. At FS 4795, turn left, and proceed as above.

Thielsen View is about 110 miles northeast of Medford, 90 miles east of Roseburg, and 15 miles north of Crater Lake.

KEY INFORMATION

Thielsen View Campground
c/o Diamond Lake Ranger District
HC 60, Box 101
Idleyld Park, OR 97447

Operated by: Umpqua National Forest

Information: (541) 498-2531

Open: May 15 to October 15

Individual sites: 60

Each site has: Picnic table, fire pit, piped water

Site assignment: First come, first served; no reservations

Registration: Self-registration on site

Facilities: Vault toilets, piped water; limited disabled access; boat dock and rentals nearby; store nearby

Parking: At individual sites

Fee: $7 per night; $3 each additional vehicle; $10 multiple-use for first 2 vehicles

Elevation: 5,200 feet

Restrictions:

Pets–On leash

Fires–In fire pits only

Alcoholic beverages–Permitted

Vehicles–RVs and trailers up to 30 feet

TRAIL BRIDGE CAMPGROUND

McKenzie Bridge, Oregon

Think of Trail Bridge as the ultimate scenic drive, complete with campground. You can make it as short as 130 miles if your starting point is Redmond, or quite a bit longer if you are coming from points west and want to make more than a frenetic weekend of it.

The drive takes you along one of Oregon's most prized trout streams, over two historic and scenic mountain passes, through a diverse assortment of picturesque landscapes ranging from alpine meadows to high desert grasslands, past many unusual geologic formations, across two of the state's largest national forests, and between two designated wildernesses.

To get there, begin the trip either in Eugene or Redmond on State Route 126 (McKenzie Highway). The focal point of this excursion is between the towns of McKenzie Bridge and Sisters over State Routes 126, 20, and 242. You'll be better off if you simply remember these three road numbers (or have a state map with you) because the road names—McKenzie Highway, Santiam Highway, Belknap Springs Highway—don't always correspond to the same piece of road continuously.

At any rate, the McKenzie River is the main feature in the western sector of the drive. Trail Bridge Campground is located on Trail Bridge Reservoir, a small

CAMPGROUND RATINGS

Beauty:	★★★
Site privacy:	★★★
Site spaciousness:	★★★
Quiet:	★★★
Security:	★★★
Cleanliness/upkeep:	★★★★
Insect control:	★★★★

Looking for a scenic drive with a convenient campground along the way? A trip to Oregon cannot be considered complete until you have driven the McKenzie River Loop.

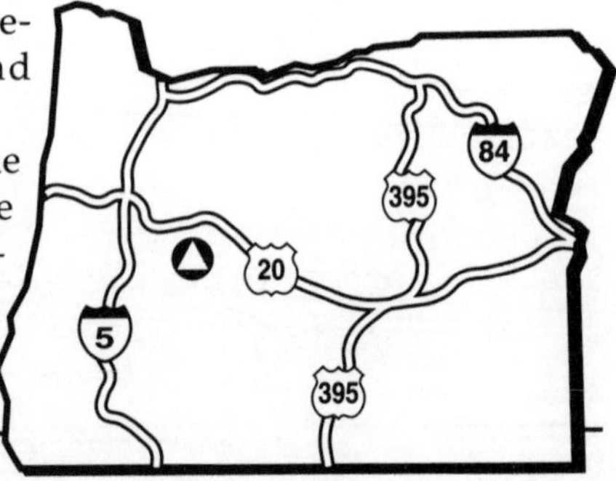

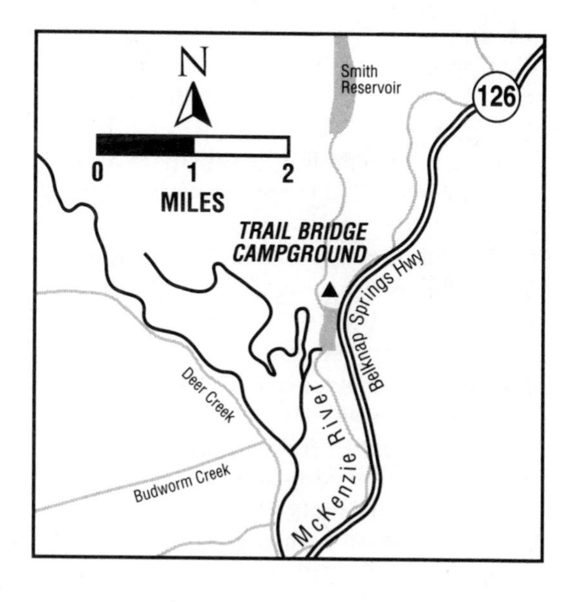

depository of McKenzie River headwaters and a good stopping point in the journey.

Flowing pure and cold out of Clear Lake (a natural lava-dam lake just west of lava beds contained within Mount Jefferson Wilderness), the McKenzie River attracts both the drift boat community and vast numbers of rafters, kayakers, and canoeists who appreciate the McKenzie's gentle grade. In the entire boatable length of the river, there is only one Class IV rapid. The rest are Class I or II.

Fishing the McKenzie can induce even the toughest angler to near-poetic descriptions of his or her experience. Besides healthy runs of summer steelhead and spring chinook and a constant supply of hatchery rainbows, the McKenzie is idolized for its native son, the redside rainbow trout. In order to keep this species alive and flourishing in its natural environs, fishing regulations require that all rainbows over 14 inches be released. Native trout are identified by their ventral fin still intact; hatchery varieties will have theirs clipped. If you plan to do some fishing, check with authorities on current regulations.

Taking Belknap Springs Highway (continuing as State Route 26), north from McKenzie Bridge, you'll encounter Trail Bridge Reservoir and the campground. If you choose to do the loop in reverse, turn right just before Belknap Springs onto State Route 242, which is the continuation of McKenzie Highway. Here the road leaves the McKenzie and picks up the western border of Three Sisters Wilderness Area as it works its way along a series of hair-raising, hairpin turns to 5,342-foot McKenzie Pass.

Continuing east, the road drops down into Sisters, a ranch town prospering largely on tourism these days, with its unlimited recreational opportunities, moderate climate, and beautiful scenery.

At Sisters, you'll catch up with the other half of SR 126, and you can continue straight across Redmond. To finish the loop and to return to Trail Bridge Campground, turn northwest onto Santiam Highway (SR 126/U.S. 20). Black Butte, a prominent natural point of interest with Metolius Spring at its base (see Riverside Campground chapter), is about 8 miles up the road on the right.

The road swings due west just beyond Black Butte, crossing Santiam Pass in about 6 more miles. The old Santiam Wagon Road was an alternative to the McKenzie Pass route for pioneers heading farther north. If you hike Pacific Crest Trail south from its intersection with U.S. 20 for about 5 miles, you'll come to the original old road.

The final part of the loop turns southwest at Santiam Junction (roughly 6 miles from the pass) and then due south on SR 126 (Belknap Springs Highway), passing Fish Lake, Clear Lake, Smith Reservoir, and a series of falls.

To get there, take SR 126 from Eugene or Redmond to McKenzie Bridge. Follow this road north; it becomes SR 26 (the continuation of Belknap Springs Highway) in McKenzie Bridge. Continue driving to Trail Bridge Reservoir and the campground.

KEY INFORMATION

Trail Bridge Campground
c/o McKenzie Ranger District
57600 McKenzie Highway
McKenzie Bridge, OR 97413

Operated by: Willamette National Forest

Information: (541) 822-3381

Open: May to October (trout fishing year-round)

Individual sites: 20 tent sites; 21 sites for RVs

Each site has: Picnic table, fire grill, shade trees

Site assignment: First come, first served; no reservations

Registration: Self-registration on site

Facilities: Vault and flush toilets; piped water; firewood; boat dock nearby; limited disabled access

Parking: At individual sites

Fee: $6 per night; $3 each additional vehicle

Elevation: 2,400 feet

Restrictions:

Pets–On leash

Fires–In fire pits only

Alcoholic beverages–Permitted

Vehicles–Separate sites for RVs; no limit on length

Other–Check for fishing regulations

OREGON CAMPGROUNDS

EASTERN OREGON

BADGER LAKE CAMPGROUND

Bennett Pass, Oregon

Okay. Call me a masochist if you want. You may have noticed by now that I seem to have a penchant for going out of my way to find campgrounds that nearly require an airlift into them. Well, Badger Lake Campground is no exception. I'll say it right now. The last stretch of the final Forest Service road (there are three of them) is intended only for high-clearance vehicles. Considering the number of fancy four-wheelers that I see crawling over the hillsides of the Northwest these days, this is not to suggest that you will be by your lonesome once you get to this high-altitude gem. However, the campground accommodates a tents-only style of camping, so revel as much as you want in the noticeable lack of RVs.

Once upon a time, Badger Lake was accessible only by a steep hike up from a trailhead on State Route 35. I'm not entirely sure why (or if) the Forest Service considers its road access an improvement over the trail. You may wonder the same thing as you navigate the roughly (and rough!) 10 miles on Forest Service roads from the turnoff at Bennett Pass. A good map of the area should prevent any unnecessary backtracking. A ranger station at Mount Hood can help with this.

Hiking is the best way to enjoy the scenic beauty of this area. The campground itself sits on the northeast edge of Badger Lake in a nonwilderness cor-

CAMPGROUND RATINGS

Beauty:	★★★★★
Site privacy:	★★★
Site spaciousness:	★★★
Quiet:	★★★ (summer)
	★★★★★ (off-season)
Security:	★★★★★
Cleanliness/upkeep:	★★★
Insect control:	★★

Hard to get to and even then accessible only in a high-clearance vehicle, the dramatic beauty of this place is worth all the trouble.

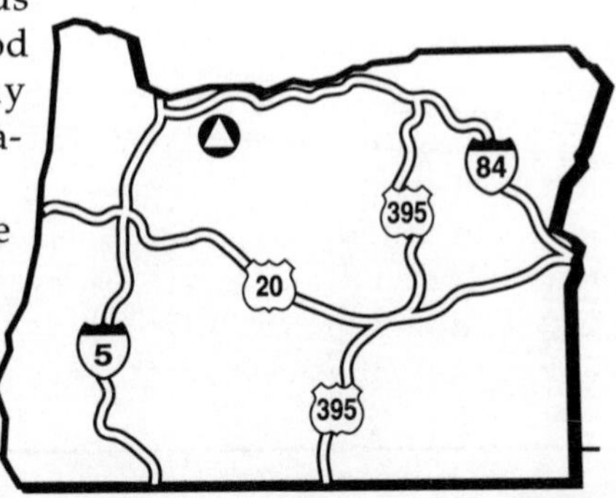

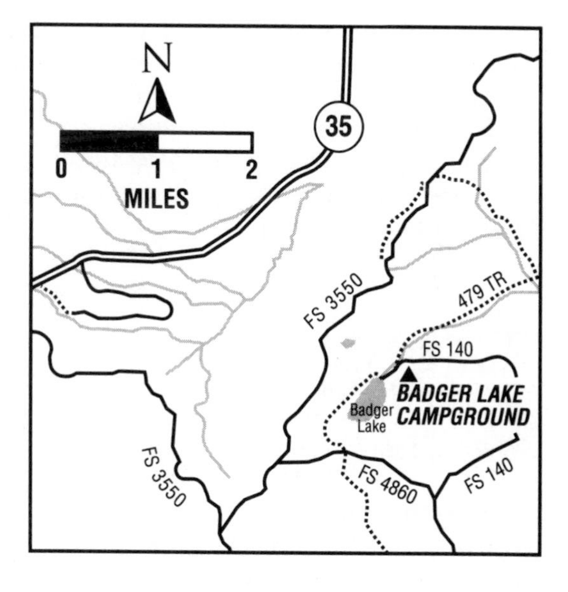

ridor adjacent to Badger Creek Wilderness. This is one of the smallest designated wildernesses in Oregon, with only 35 square miles of protected lands. But within this tiny plot are geographic transitions and climatic changes of dramatic proportions unlikely to be found in any other comparably sized stretch of Oregon country.

In this unique microcosm, where forested mountains meet dusty lowlands, nearly 70 inches of precipitation fall on the western ridges compared to only 20 inches in the eastern sector. Old-growth Douglas fir is gradually replaced by the unusual appearance of ponderosa and white pine together. For some unexplainable reason, these two tree types are found together only in brief stretches on both sides of the Columbia River at about the same longitudinal point. In Oregon, they grow between Hood River and The Dalles.

For the best views of this land in transition (as well as vistas of mighty Mount Hood), hike to the top of 6,525-foot Lookout Mountain. Numerous other trails lead into the backcountry to such destinations as Gumjuwac Saddle, Gunsight Butte, and Flag Point. The Divide Trail between Lookout Mountain and Flag Point looks down on the canyons of Badger Creek for glimpses of dramatic cliffs and rock formations. Wildflowers such as penstemon, Indian paintbrush, and avalanche lily are at their prime in the eastern portion of the wilderness until late July, at which time the colorful displays jump to higher elevations in the west. In total, roughly 80 miles of trails traverse Badger Creek Wilderness with connecting routes into Mount Hood Wilderness to the north and west.

Located as it is on the eastern slopes of the Cascades at 4,472 feet, Badger Lake and adjacent trails are usually not snow free until mid-June and stay clear at least through mid-September. Although heavy snow prohibits travel into this high country in winter, Nordic skiers can take advantage of plowed roads from Bennett Pass southeast toward the wilderness boundary. SR 35 is kept open all winter to accommodate alpine skiers heading for Mount Hood's facilities. Boating on Badger Lake is possible if you didn't lose your canoes on the way in. There's good rainbow and brook trout fishing. The White River Paddle Route farther south along the old Barlow Road (formerly a wagon route for settlers) is another boating option.

To get there from the town of Mount Hood (14 miles south of Hood River), travel south on SR 35 for approximately 20 miles to FS 3550. Turn left and at about 6 miles, turn left onto FS 4860. In 2 miles, turn left again onto FS 140, and follow it to the campground.

KEY INFORMATION

Badger Lake Campground
c/o Barlow Ranger District
P.O. Box 67
Dufur, OR 97021

Operated by: Mount Hood National Forest

Information: (541) 467-2291

Open: July to September

Individual sites: 15

Some sites have: Picnic table, fire grill, shade trees

Site assignment: First come, first served; no reservations

Registration: Self-registration on site

Facilities: Pit toilets, no piped water

Parking: At individual sites

Fee: No fee

Elevation: 4,472 feet

Restrictions:

Pets–On leash

Fires–In fire pits only

Alcoholic beverages–Permitted

Vehicles–No RVs or trailers, high-clearance vehicles recommended; nonmotorized boats only

BEAVERTAIL CAMPGROUND

Maupin, Oregon

Primitive. Desolate. Rugged. Wild. Haunting. These are a few of the adjectives that quickly come to mind when I think back to my first impressions of Deschutes River country. *"Riviere des Chutes"* (River of the Falls), as it was originally named by French trappers for the Hudson Bay Company, is the hallowed waterway of central Oregon's high desert.

Flowing north out of Lava Lake just south of Mount Bachelor, the Deschutes (pronounced *de shoot*) travels toward its confluence with the mighty Columbia River under the protective aegis of state and federal legislation. This is Oregon's second longest river, and it has such a remarkable transformation from its docile beginnings above Wickiup Reservoir to a thundering torrent downstream that it has prompted separate references of Upper Deschutes and Lower Deschutes.

Upper Deschutes (from headwaters to Bend) has been honored with inclusion in the Oregon Scenic Waterway Program for its picturesque, recreational, and natural qualities. Its subtle charms are often overshadowed, however, by its tempestuous lower half and the focus of this campground entry.

The Lower Deschutes River is by far the more popular of the two sections, coming under Wild and Scenic protection in 1988. Its untamed whitewater, steep basalt canyon walls, native trout and steel-

CAMPGROUND RATINGS

Beauty:	★★★★★
Site privacy:	★★★
Site spaciousness:	★★★★
Quiet:	★★ (summer)
	★★★ (off-season)
Security:	★★
Cleanliness/upkeep:	★★★
Insect control:	★★★

This is bare-bones camping at its best: the sky, the sand, the river, and thou. What more could you wish?

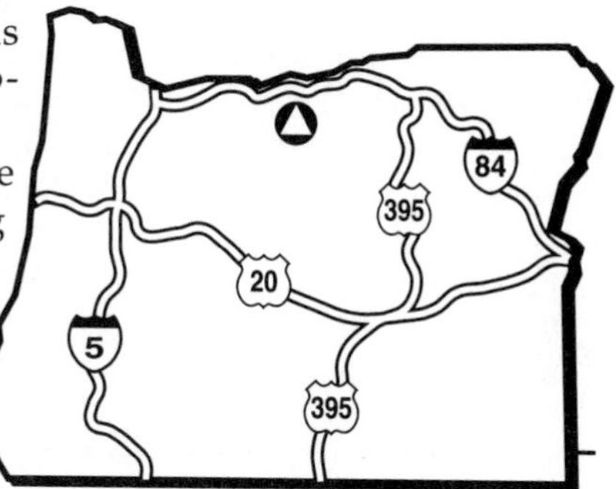

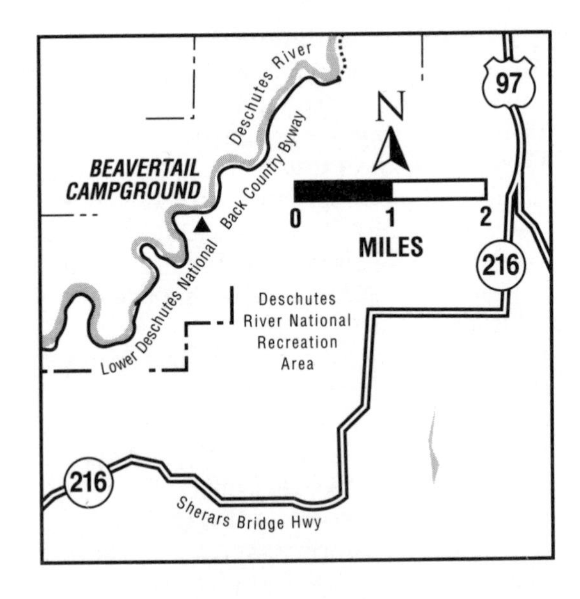

head, and historic intrigue attract an eclectic array of recreational users from near and far. The Wild and Scenic status is the river's best insurance that its unspoiled existence will continue indefinitely for all to enjoy.

Today, Beavertail Campground is one of several minimally developed sites along the eastern bank of the Lower Deschutes that are provided in classic Bureau of Land Management style. You've heard the phrase, "Less is more?" It could easily be the Bureau of Land Management's motto.

In all truthfulness, the Bureau knew what it was doing when it created Beavertail. Views across the water from the riverside compound encompass some of the Lower Deschutes' most spectacular basalt rimrock canyon walls. Cedar Island is just downstream, so named for a misplaced stand of incense cedar that usually grows farther west in the Cascades. So photographers, grab your gear and find a comfortable spot amongst the shore grasses. The kayaks and rafts will be bobbing around the bend any minute.

Speaking of boating, the 51-mile trip from Maupin to the Columbia via the Deschutes is by permit only (available at local sporting goods stores in central Oregon). For the experienced paddler, there are three Class IV rapids, dozens of less technical ones for the novices, and one that is in a class all by itself. It's known as Sherar's Falls, and the classification is "portage." The falls are still in use today by Warm Springs Indians and other local Native Americans who dipnet for trout and spawning salmon from rickety platforms that teeter precariously over the raging spillway below.

I watched in awe for nearly an hour one day as a veteran of this ages-old practice pulled up a fish about every ten minutes and clubbed it senseless with one swift bash of a giant wooden stick. Lashing the dipnet back into position first, he then gutted each fish with lightning speed and carefully packed it in a blanket of ice.

The climate in this rugged wildwater backcountry is, as you may have guessed, as extreme as the terrain. Summers can be very hot (90s and 100s), while winters generally drop below freezing. The Bureau of Land Management lands are open all year, so make sure you have all the appropriate emergency supplies depending on your choice of season. Gusty winds and sudden thunderstorms are commonplace.

The road that accesses Beavertail and all other Bureau dispersed and managed sites is known as the Lower Deschutes National Back Country Byway. This thoroughfare can be quite crowded in summer, especially on weekends. Use caution if you choose to explore by mountain bike.

To get there from Maupin (42 miles south of The Dalles on US 197), follow Deschutes River Road north along the east bank of the Deschutes River for approximately 18 miles to the campground.

KEY INFORMATION

Beavertail Campground
c/o Prineville District Office
P.O. Box 550
Prineville, OR 97754

Operated by: Bureau of Land Management

Information: (541) 447-4115

Open: All year

Individual sites: 20

Some sites have: Picnic table, fire grill, shade trees

Site assignment: First come, first served; no reservations

Registration: Self-registration on site

Facilities: Vault toilets, piped water, boat launch nearby

Parking: At individual sites

Fee: $3 per night, $1 for each additional vehicle

Elevation: 1,200 feet

Restrictions:

Pets–On leash

Fires–In fire pits only and according to seasonal restrictions

Alcoholic beverages–Permitted

Vehicles–Driving on vegetation not allowed

Other–Boating by permit only

FOURMILE LAKE CAMPGROUND

Klamath Falls, Oregon

Views of a 9,500-foot snowcapped peak. Spacious, lakefront tent sites wonderfully free of annoying mosquitoes. A wilderness boundary veritably at the backflap of your tent. Trailheads to some of the wildest high-elevation territory in Oregon. A huge national wildlife refuge less than 20 miles away. Regular security patrols. The services of civilization within an hour's drive.

It's hard to beat this glowing set of credentials that is part of the package when you stay at Fourmile Lake Campground in Winema National Forest.

Although Fourmile's campsites are sizable enough to accommodate RVs and the like, the general sense of the place is one of solitude and serenity. This is due, in part, to the proximity of Sky Lakes Wilderness, whose boundary is outlined by nearly three-fourths of the lake's shoreline.

Creating this squiggly crook in the wilderness's otherwise linear demarcation, Fourmile Lake itself is not within the protected boundaries, and motorized boat travel (with speed limit enforced) is acceptable. Any form of mechanized transportation within the wilderness territory is, however, strictly prohibited.

As always when hiking into wilderness backcountry, it is a good idea to carry a compass and a detailed USGS topographic map of the area. Forest Service

CAMPGROUND RATINGS

Beauty:	★★★★
Site privacy:	★★★
Site spaciousness:	★★★★★
Quiet:	★★★★
Security:	★★★★
Cleanliness/upkeep:	★★★★★
Insect control:	★★★★

If you're campground shopping in the southern Oregon Cascades, it's hard to beat these fabulous views, lakefront sites, and wilderness trails.

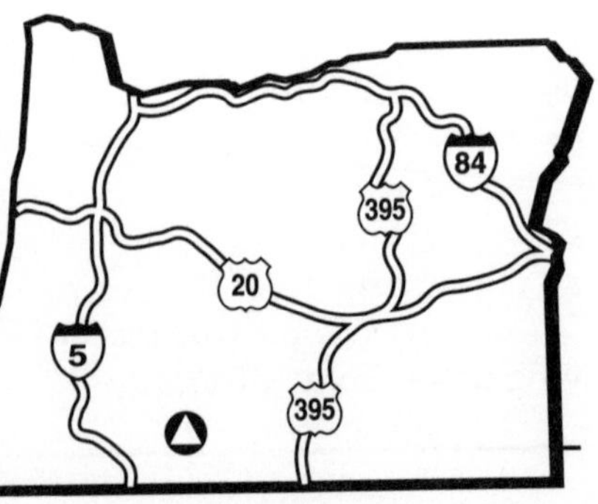

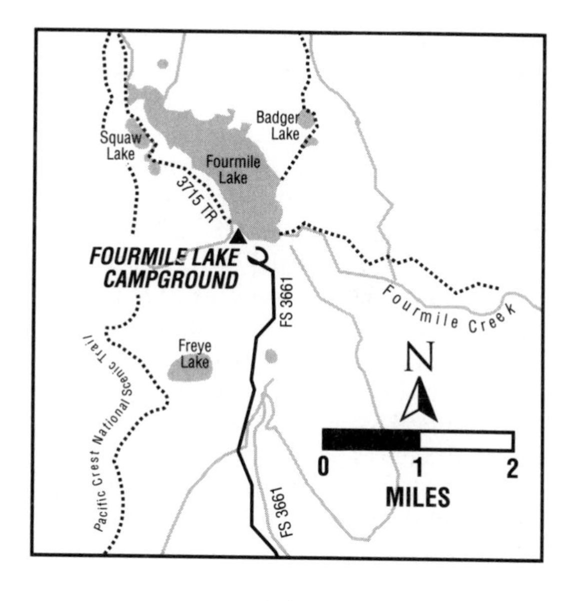

maps are generally reliable but are often not updated frequently enough to reflect the most recent additions or changes in their vast network of roads. Try to get the most current information from a Forest Service representative. They're very friendly and helpful in Klamath Falls.

Since hiking and backpacking are requirements for enjoying this area properly, consider your options in either Sky Lakes Wilderness or Mountain Lakes Wilderness. Trails into Sky Lakes leave very near the campground. The one to the northwest bypasses little Squaw Lake (where views of Mount McLoughlin will make you stop and gape) and soon thereafter connects with the Pacific Crest National Scenic Trail (about 2 miles from the campground). From there, you could hike south on the Pacific Crest Trail to its junction with the Mount McLoughlin Trail (a difficult but nontechnical climb).The summit is about 3 miles from this point. The total length of this trip from campground to peak top would make for a rather rigorous 14-mile, round-trip day hike. The alternative is to hike the Mount McLoughlin Trail from its trailhead on FS 3650. An elevation gain of 4,000 feet doesn't make the trip any easier, but it is shorter (10 miles round-trip).

Be sure to read the brochure that is provided at the trailhead. It covers some necessary precautions that can make the difference between delight and disaster on this fourth-highest Oregon peak.

To experience the true essence of Sky Lakes Wilderness, I recommend driving to the Cold Springs trailhead on FS 3651. Saunter into the heart of this magnificent area with Imagination Peak as your inspiration. Beginning at an altitude of 5,800 feet, the trail climbs gently up and down with minimal elevation gain or loss.

In about 6 miles, you'll come to Heavenly Twin Lakes and the turnaround point if you're just out for the day. This is a good spot to see osprey that travel from nesting areas up to 8 miles away to fish in the hundreds of lakes scattered in this alpine basin. The trail wanders north past more peaks and more lakes until it catches up with the Pacific Crest Trail as it works its way toward Crater Lake National Park.

A challenging side trip if you have the four-wheel rig for it is up Pelican Butte (also accessed from FS 3651). The Forest Service has a permanent lookout station here, but the road is not maintained for normal-clearance vehicles.

For a closer look at the array of wildlife and waterfowl that inhabit the 15,000 acres of refuge, rent a canoe down on Pelican Bay and follow Upper Klamath Canoe Trail through 6 miles of lake and marshland.

To get there, take State Route 140 (Lake of the Woods Highway) northwest out of Klamath Falls for 38 miles, then turn right onto FS 3661, and head north for 5.5 miles to the campground.

To get there from Medford, head east on SR 140 for 40 miles. From this direction, you will turn left onto FS 3661.

KEY INFORMATION

Fourmile Lake Campground
c/o Klamath Ranger District
1936 California Avenue
Klamath Falls, OR 97601

Operated by: Winema National Forest

Information: (541) 883-6824

Open: June 10 to October 15, weather permitting

Individual sites: 21

Each site has: Picnic table, fire pit with grill, shade trees

Site assignment: First come, first served; no reservations

Registration: Self-registration on site

Facilities: Pit toilets, central handpump for water, boat launch, firewood

Parking: At individual sites

Fee: $5 per night, $2 each additional vehicle

Elevation: 5,800 feet

Restrictions:

Pets–On leash

Fires–In fire pits only

Alcoholic beverages–Permitted

Vehicles–Not allowed in wilderness area; nonmotorized boats only

Other–14-day limit on stay

HAT POINT CAMPGROUND

Hells Canyon, Oregon

One hell of a hole in the ground! That's how geologists have described the awesome spectacle of Hells Canyon, the deepest, erosion-carved river canyon in North America. Once you've peered down from the 6,982-foot Hat Point Lookout into this seemingly bottomless chasm, you'll agree that it is a most fitting description.

One must be prepared to explore Hells Canyon and the Wild and Scenic Snake River in one of three ways: by foot, by hoof, or by boat. Hat Point and the few primitive campgrounds nearby are within the boundaries of Hells Canyon (accessible by road), but beyond Hat Point, the designation is wilderness and roads are unheard of.

There are, however, 1,000 miles of trails that traverse more than 200,000 acres of snowy mountain peaks, forested ridges, grassy benchlands, jagged rimrock, and sandy canyon floors. These trails are maintained to varying degrees and test a variety of skill levels. Check with the Wallowa-Whitman National Forest staff on trail conditions when planning your intra-wilderness itinerary. Forest Service headquarters are in Baker City, with district ranger offices in Enterprise, Joseph, Unity, La Grande, and Halfway. Hells Canyon National Recreation Area has its headquarters in Enterprise, with branch offices in Idaho.

CAMPGROUND RATINGS

Beauty:	★★★★★
Site privacy:	★★★
Site spaciousness:	★★★★
Quiet:	★★★ (summer)
	★★★★★ (off-season)
Security:	★★★
Cleanliness/upkeep:	★★★
Insect control:	★★★

This is a lonely and desolately beautiful place; one that requires a bit of thought and advance planning to enjoy its natural wonders adequately and safely.

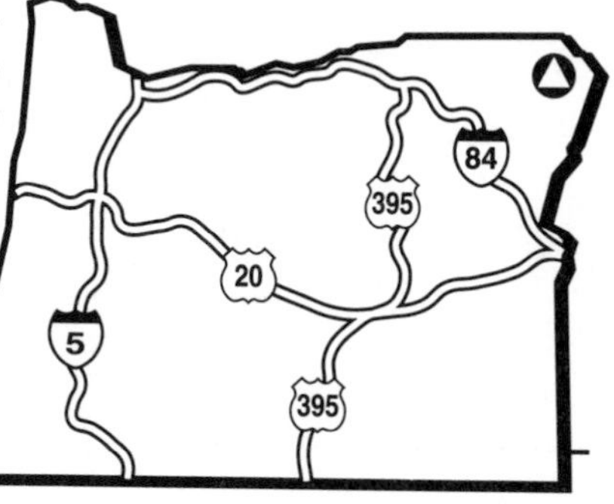

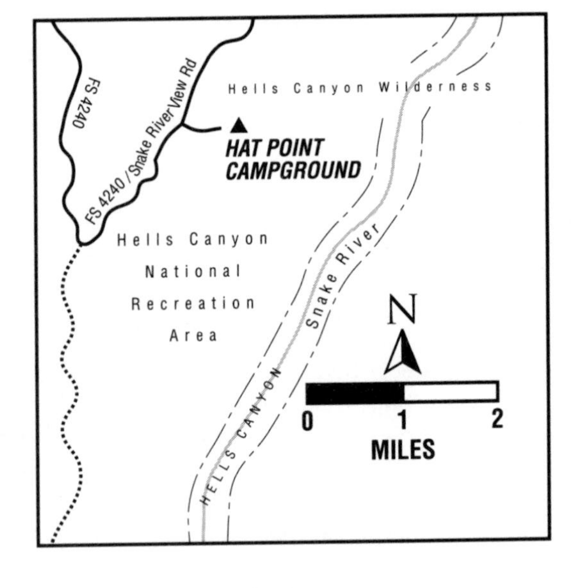

If you prefer to see Hells Canyon by way of the Snake River, contact any of the Forest Service or National Recreation Area offices mentioned to get information on reservations, restrictions, and permits. Regulations vary, depending on time of year and the kind of boating to be done. These agencies will also have up-to-date lists of outfitters who can take you into the heart of this magnificent territory by pack horse.

Once upon a time, part of the adventure of Hells Canyon was just getting to Hat Point. This experience will be lost on first-time visitors now due to major rehabilitation efforts over the past several years. Previously, Forest Service Road 4240 from the town of Imnaha to Hat Point was a tortuously rutted affair that ate up low-clearance vehicles and took even the hardiest drivers nearly three hours to travel the 24-mile distance. An improved road was completed in the summer of 1992.

A better road can only mean more people. While this will have an effect on Hat Point's once-remote nature, perhaps it will encourage the Forest Service to realize that Hells Canyon's future should be recreation, not resources.

Whatever method of travel you choose within Hells Canyon Wilderness or Hells Canyon National Recreation Area or in the Wild and Scenic Snake River corridor, please keep in mind that dramatic changes in elevation—from 1,000 feet up to 9,300—create a full range of microclimates with corresponding weather conditions, wildlife habitats, and vegetation environments.

All can be encountered in a single outing as you descend from the breezy alpine heights of Hat Point brimming with seasonal wildflowers to the hot, often windless riverside lowlands where prickly pear cactus thrives.

The nearest piped water to Hat Point is at the Memaloose Landing Strip. Saddle Creek Campground is an alternative to Hat Point, with seven tent sites and an observation area. It is as undeveloped as Hat Point. Sacajawea Campground suffered fire damage in 1988, and there are no plans at the present time to restore it.

This is rattlesnake country in the summertime. If you plan either short or long trips into the wilderness, a snakebite kit is strongly recommended. It's a long way out to services and medical help.

To get there from Imnaha (36 miles east of Enterprise), travel southeast on FS 4240 (Hat Point Road) to the campground and lookout tower. Keep to the right fork just past Memaloose Landing Strip; FS 4240 continues as Snake River View Road.

KEY INFORMATION

Hat Point Campground
c/o Hells Canyon National Recreation Area
P.O. Box 490
Enterprise, OR 97828

Operated by: Wallowa-Whitman National Forest

Information: (541) 785-3395

Open: July to late November

Individual sites: 6

Each site has: Picnic table, fire pit with grill

Site assignment: First come, first served; no reservations

Registration: Not necessary

Facilities: Vault toilets, no piped water, horse ramp

Parking: At individual sites

Fee: No fee

Elevation: 6,900 feet

Restrictions:

Pets–On leash

Fires–In fire pits only

Alcoholic beverages–Permitted

Vehicles–No RVs or trailers

EAST

HEAD OF THE RIVER CAMPGROUND

Chiloquin, Oregon

We were sitting in a coffee shop in Klamath Falls, hard on the campground research trail. Besides the aroma of fresh-ground French roast opening up my drowsy, sleep-stagnant sinuses, there was the unmistakable scent of a soon-to-be-discovered secret campground. You know, the ones that the locals are afraid to admit to either because the Forest Service will get wind of it and "undevelop" the hell out of it or some sly, yuppie, pseudo-outdoors person (hey, not me!) will want to include it in a damn guidebook, and there goes the neighborhood.

Right on both counts in the case of this choice offering. How do I get so lucky? You learn to recognize the signals quickly.

So there we were in the coffee shop swilling our fair share of java. "Say, you wouldn't happen to know of any great little out-of-the-way camping spots around here, would you?" I asked innocently, with my nose stuck in a steaming mug.

The place wasn't all that crowded so it was obvious to the fellow behind the counter that the question was meant for him. He looked up with the tiniest twist of a smile, cocked his head to the side in exaggerated contemplation, pursed his lips, and said, "What do you mean by 'out of the way?'"

I'll spare you the details of the conversation, but the upshot was this dandy

CAMPGROUND RATINGS

Beauty:	★★★★
Site privacy:	★★ ½
Site spaciousness:	★★★★
Quiet:	★★★★
Security:	★★
Cleanliness/upkeep:	★★★
Insect control:	★★★

A great little out-of-the-way place where you'll run into more wildlife than fellow campers.

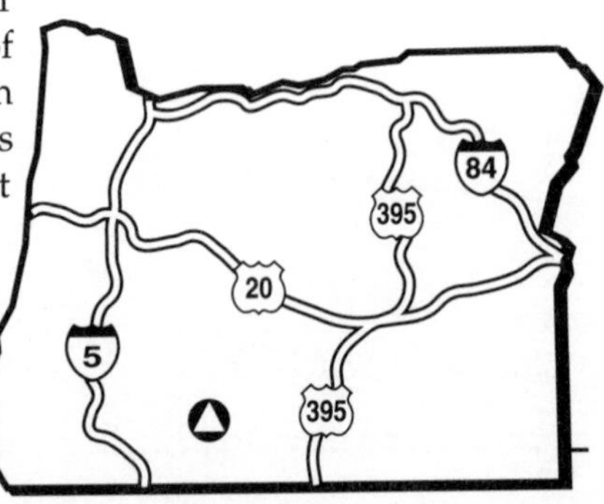

little spot known as Head of the River Campground.

Lo and behold, I have actually seen it listed in a few other campground guides, so I guess I wasn't the first to play that game with the Klamath coffee connoisseur. Must have some arrangement with the Forest Service.

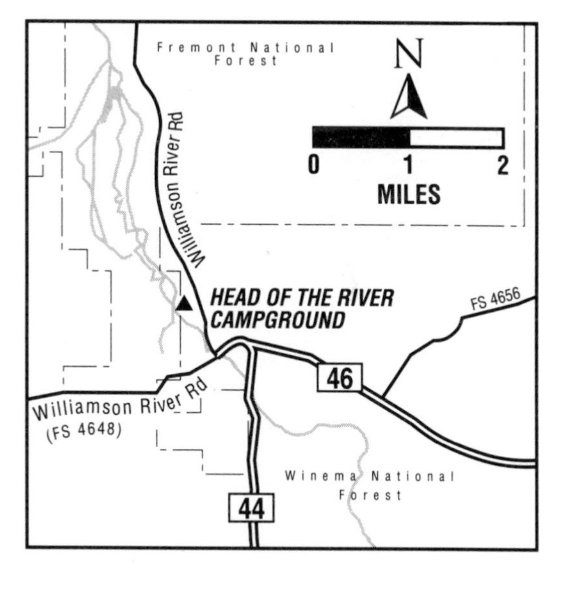

There is not much out here on this tableland of ponderosa pine, lodgepole pine, and assorted conifers except a bit of excellent trout fishing in the Williamson River and a crazy contingent of Forest Service roads that wander in and around the numerous buttes and flats. The Forest Service would like to encourage more recreational use of these roads. For the most part, they are used heavily by loggers.

This area is relatively dry year-round, and the only substantial precipitation comes in the form of snow at higher elevations. However, there is enough groundwater seeping to the surface from natural springs that wildflowers, such as fireweed, foxglove, lupine, and dandelion, define the banks of tiny creeks that quickly dry up after spring.

You'll most likely encounter more wildlife than fellow campers out here in upper Williamson country. More than 230 species of birds and 80 varieties of mammals inhabit the region. In the summer months, watch out for rattlesnakes and bring your mosquito repellent. Carry your own drinking water to the Head of the River or be prepared to treat what you take from the river.

Rather than backtracking along the route you took to get to this pristine spot, you can consider a loop trip by continuing north on Williamson River Road, which becomes Silver Lake Road just above the expansive Klamath

Marsh. You can get a bird's eye view of Klamath Forest National Wildlife Refuge because Silver Lake Road cuts a diagonal across the refuge's midsection to a juncture with U.S. 97 at Chinchalo. This could easily be one of the least-traveled byways you'll find in this book.

For more specifics on the area, see what the information officer at the Chiloquin Ranger District office can tell you.

To get there, take Sprague River Highway (OR 858) northeast out of Chiloquin. Take a left onto Williamson River Highway at a little more than the 5-mile point. Follow this road 27 miles to the access road, FS 4648. Take a left onto FS 4648; the campground is 1 mile on the left. Signs for the campground begin at the turn for FS 4648.

KEY INFORMATION

Head of the River Campground
c/o Chiloquin Ranger District
P.O. Box 357
Chiloquin, OR 97624

Operated by: Winema National Forest

Information: (541) 783-2221

Open: June to October, depending on weather

Individual sites: 6

Each site has: Fire grill

Some sites have: Picnic table, shade trees

Site assignment: First come, first served; no reservations

Registration: Not necessary

Facilities: Vault toilets, firewood, no piped water

Parking: At individual sites

Fee: No fee

Elevation: 4,500 feet

Restrictions:

Pets–On leash

Fires–In designated areas only

Alcoholic beverages–Permitted

Vehicles–RVs and trailers up to 30 feet

LOST CREEK CAMPGROUND

Crater Lake, Oregon

When the lodge at Crater Lake National Park reopens in 1994 after major renovation and restoration, the campground of this listing will be less crowded than usual.

Generally, Lost Creek Campground with its tents-only accommodations is an ideal spot for a base camp just far enough out of the way of the heavily trafficked areas and the only other campground in the park, Mazama. Located much closer to the main southern entrance to the park, Mazama is recognizable as the one where all the RVs are turning off.

Get to Lost Creek as early as possible in the summertime. Even though it's a bit off the beaten path, this area is still swarming with people looking for overnight accommodations.

The camping season at Crater Lake can be quite short, owing to its high-altitude at roughly 7,000 feet. Lost Creek Campground sits at 6,000 feet, and with normal snowfalls averaging 550 inches (yep, that's 45 feet!), the East Rim Drive is often not open until mid-July.

Crater Lake is a stupendous natural wonder, no matter what the weather conditions may be. If this is your first trip to Crater Lake National Park, be prepared to have your jaw drop when you take your first peek over the rim of this massive caldera.

CAMPGROUND RATINGS

Beauty:	★★★★
Site privacy:	★★★★★
Site spaciousness:	★★★★★
Quiet:	★★★★★
Security:	★★★
Cleanliness/upkeep:	★★★★
Insect control:	★★★

This is the ideal base camp from which to explore Crater Lake National Park.

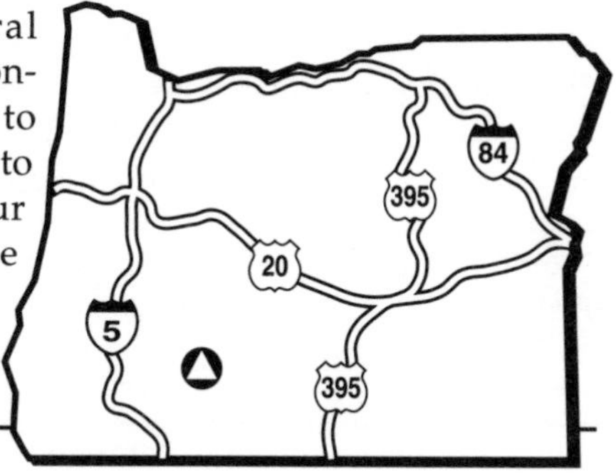

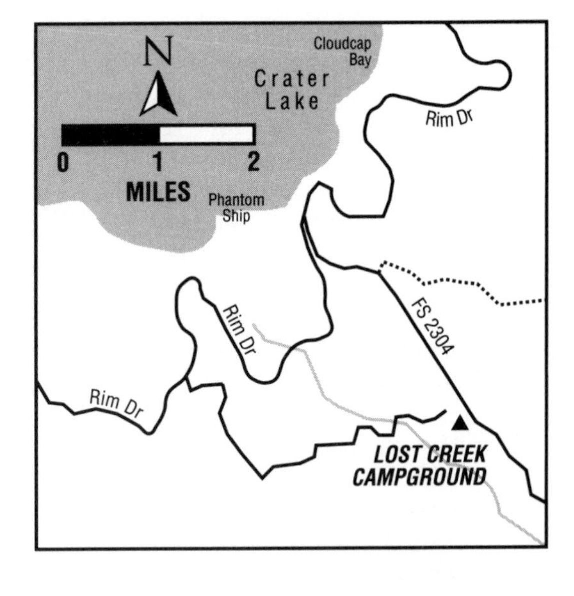

The deepest lake in the United States, the second deepest in North America, and the seventh deepest in the world, Crater Lake is the result of the cataclysmic eruption of Mount Mazama some 6,850 years ago. It once was a stratovolcano similar to Mount Hood and Mount Shasta and stood roughly a mile higher than the current lake level before it collapsed.

There are several excellent publications about Crater Lake, Mount Mazama, and the park at the visitor center in Rim Village. I found it helpful to have these along as I toured the area. It's the kind of place where a little knowledge can make an immensely more pleasurable trip.

Rim Drive circumnavigates the perimeter of the 6-mile-wide lake for a driving distance of 33.4 miles. There are numerous viewpoints along the way that will slow the driving time, but figure roughly two hours to complete the loop. In the winter, Rim Drive is open only between park headquarters and Rim Village, accessed by way of State Route 62 either from the west or south. In all seasons, the Rim Drive is open to mountain bikes, but there is no shoulder—so be careful!

Recreational activities in the 183,277 acres of Crater Lake National Park border on exhaustive. At this altitude, that might well read "exhausting." There are more than 140 miles of hiking trails, including a section of the Pacific Crest National Scenic Trail, and some trail heights can reach close to 9,000 feet. That height can take its toll on unconditioned legs and the unacclimatized cardiovascular system.

Hiking, however, is really the best way to enjoy Crater Lake National Park. Solitude on the trail is one of the hallmarks of Crater Lake, unlike many other national parks that suffer the "take-a-number" style of outdoor recreation.

The diverse wildlife and plant life in this part of Oregon is fascinating to observe firsthand. Whether by the brilliant green mosses at Thousand Springs, the spongy meadowlands of Sphagnum Bog, or bald eagles circling over snow-blanketed crags, the naturalist in you will be inspired to strike out for the lonelier parts of the park.

For the geologist in you, there are destinations such as The Pinnacles (close to camp) and similarly weird formations on the Godfrey Glen Trail. The Pumice Desert is on the north side of the park, and Wizard Island, the small, symmetrical volcanic cone protruding from the lake, is accessible by boat from Cleetwood Cove. It's a steep, 720-foot drop just over a mile down to the cove. The way down may seem manageable enough, but after several hours of hiking on Wizard Island, that last mile back up may be the most memorable. Leave enough time at day's end to make the ascent in daylight.

To get there, enter Crater Lake National Park and continue past Mazama Campground to Rim Drive. Take the east rim route, and turn right at Kerr Notch toward The Pinnacles. Lost Creek Campground is adjacent to tiny Lost Creek several miles down this road.

KEY INFORMATION

Lost Creek Campground
Crater Lake National Park
P.O. Box 7
Crater Lake, OR 97604

Operated by: National Park Service

Information: (541) 594-2211

Open: Early July to late September, depending on snow level

Individual sites: 16

Each site has: Picnic table, fire grill

Site assignment: First come, first served; no reservations

Registration: Not necessary

Facilities: Flush toilets, piped water, group camp

Parking: At individual sites

Fee: $11 per night

Elevation: 6,000 feet

Restrictions:

Pets–On leash

Fires–In fire pits only

Alcoholic beverages–In campsite

Vehicles–Motorbikes allowed; no accommodations for RVs

PAGE SPRINGS CAMPGROUND

Frenchglen, Oregon

One look at the southeastern expanse of Oregon, roughly 60 miles south of Burns, and you know you're in a place where country-western music is as common as cornbread. Mile after dusty mile, scraggly sagebrush, twisted juniper, and jagged rimrock share a landscape punctuated only by the hulk of mile-high Steens Mountain. This is the highest fault-block mountain in the nation and a snowcapped beacon for all of southeast Oregon.

The region was once the turf of the largest cattle ranch in the United States. Pete French arrived in the Donner und Blitzen River valley in 1872 with 120 head of cattle and built an empire that totaled 45,000 cattle and 200,000 acres. Cattle operations still exist in parts of the Steens Mountain area today. But with all the natural wonders to behold, outdoor recreation and tourism are gradually replacing the traditional sources of income.

Page Springs Campground sits invitingly in the midst of this spectrum. Maintained by the Bureau of Land Management out of its Burns district office, Page Springs is one of three public campgrounds that the Bureau provides for visitors. I prefer it because it is more centrally located to interesting day trips that await in just about any direction you choose to go. It is also the only one of

CAMPGROUND RATINGS

Beauty:	★★★★
Site privacy:	★★★
Site spaciousness:	★★★
Quiet:	★★★★★
Security:	★★★★
Cleanliness/upkeep:	★★★★★
Insect control:	★

Of three Bureau of Land Management campgrounds in the Steens Mountain area, Page Springs is the more centrally located for day trips and the only one open year-round.

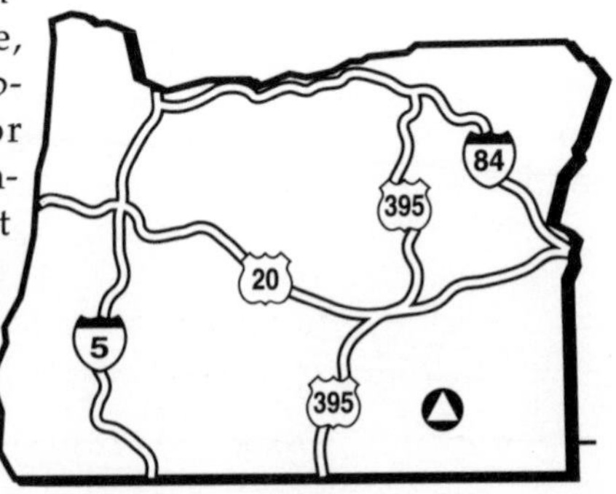

the three campgrounds that is open year-round.

Once you've settled in among the sagebrush and aspens, your first activity of choice may be the 1.8-mile walk that follows the meandering Donner und Blitzen through tall stands of surprisingly lush grasses and other vegetation. This short path is part of a longer route known as the Desert Trail that will—if the efforts of the national Desert Trail Association are successful—provide access to some of the most beautiful arid sections of North America between Canada and Mexico. Oregon's contribution to the trail network is 77 miles.

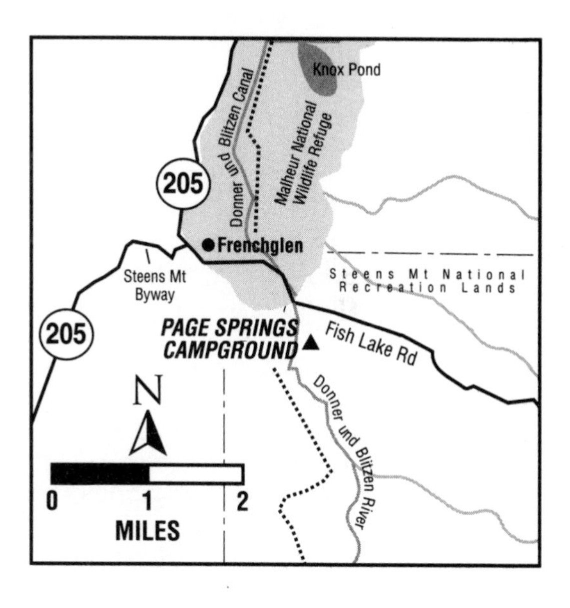

Now that you've stretched your legs and checked out the lay of the land, consider the more distant options. If you're visiting the area in summer, you may want to escape the intense, merciless heat with a drive around Steens Mountain National Back Country Byway. Be sure to fill your gas tank, and carry extra water for both you and the car. A gallon per person per day, I've heard. The road is quite rough, the entire loop distance is 66 miles, and what minimal emergency services exist are in Frenchglen, which will be well behind you once you set out. The weather can change quickly and dramatically, so be prepared for extremes of wind and precipitation. Snow is not uncommon in midsummer at higher altitudes.

One last thing: The road is not recommended for RVs.

While all this may sound a bit daunting, think about how often you have an opportunity to drive to the summit of a 9,773-foot mountain that bares so many of its geologic secrets from numerous overlooks and short hikes along the way. Witness the effects of glacial activity with such clear-cut examples as Kiger, Little Blitzen, Big Indian, and Wildhorse Gorges—massive U-shaped troughs up to a half mile deep. The mountain is a veritable living laboratory for botanists and biologists, with five distinct habitat zones ringing its slopes.

Wildlife abounds in the Steens Mountain area, and Malheur National Wildlife Refuge just north of Page Springs provides viewing areas from which as many as 280 species of birds and nearly 60 species of mammals have been observed. The refuge's 185,000 acres of lakes, ponds, marshes, and soggy meadows rank it as one of the top havens for breeding waterfowl, upland game birds, fur-bearers, and big game. Because Page Springs is open all year, bird enthusiasts should try to plan their trips to the refuge anytime from late February through May, when migratory wave after wave of winged creatures take to the skies. Tundra swans, Canada geese, lesser sandhill cranes in February; shorebirds such as willets, long-billed curlews, and avocets in April; thousands upon thousands of songbirds in May. Beware, however, of the heavy mosquito population present until midsummer.

Herds of the wild Kiger mustang, a direct descendant of the horse introduced to America by Spanish conquistadors, roam areas around the Steens.

To get there, drive south from just east of Burns on SR 205 about 60 miles to the town of Frenchglen (named in honor of the cattle baron and his equally ambitious father-in-law, Hugh Glenn). Find North Loop Steens Mountain Road, and head east about 4 miles. The campground is adjacent to the oasis-like Donner und Blitzen River.

KEY INFORMATION

Page Springs Campground
c/o Burns District Office
HC 74-12533 Highway 20 West
Hines, OR 97738

Operated by: Bureau of Land Management

Information: (541) 573-4400

Open: All year

Individual sites: 36

Some sites have: Picnic table, fire pit with grill, shade trees

Site assignment: First come, first served; no reservations

Registration: Self-registration on site

Facilities: Pit toilets, piped water, firewood, disabled access in the works

Parking: At individual sites

Fee: $4 per night, May to October

Elevation: 4,200 feet

Restrictions:

Fires–In fire pits only

Alcoholic beverages–Permitted

Vehicles–No accommodations for RVs or trailers

RIVERSIDE CAMPGROUND

Sisters, Oregon

CAMPGROUND RATINGS

Beauty:	★★★★
Site privacy:	★★★
Site spaciousness:	★★★★
Quiet:	★★★★
Security:	★★★
Cleanliness/upkeep:	★★★
Insect control:	★★★

One of many campgrounds near the fisherman's paradise that is the Metolius River—and the only one that does not charge a fee.

Ah, the magical and mysterious Metolius. Welling up clear and bright from a tiny underground spring at the base of Black Butte and providing one of the finest trout habitats around before emptying into Lake Billy Chinook.

While the Metolius River may be known for its trout today, there was a time when salmon sought its cooling waters. The word "Metolius" derives from "my-tolyas," a term that showed up in a 19th-century Pacific Railroad survey report. The reference is to a variety of salmon that is no longer found in the river.

Fishermen, on the other hand, will be in plentiful supply if you come to the Metolius at the height of the fly-fishing season. The number of campgrounds on or near the Metolius is staggering, and they are there primarily to serve the abundance of anglers. In addition to Riverside, there are Camp Sherman, Allingham, Smiling River, Pine Rest, Gorge, Allen Springs, Pioneer Ford, and Lower Bridge. All of these are managed by the Sisters Ranger District of the Deschutes National Forest, and all except Riverside require a fee. Don't ask me why, and if you're smart, you won't ask at the ranger station, either. Riverside also opens sooner and closes later (mid-April to mid-October) than the rest.

This area of central Oregon is characterized by warm—even hot—and dry

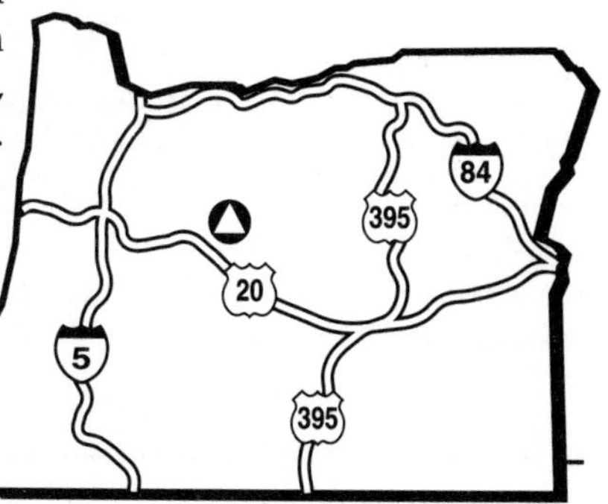

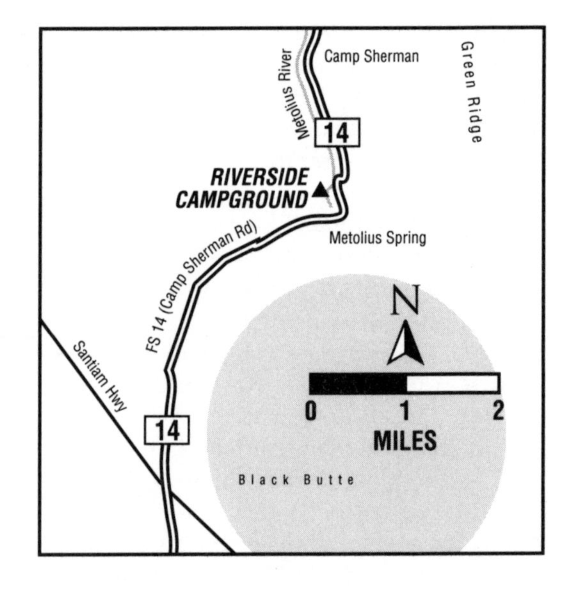

summers and cold, snowy winters. Upland areas have been known to receive as much as 20 feet of snow, and many trails will be blocked well into May. The terrain is laid with a volcanic base, out of which is created a dazzling collage of crystalline streams, creeks, and rivers; ancient lava flows; dormant and deteriorated craters; sparkling inlays of obsidian; rugged basalt cliffs; flat-topped mesas and buttes; and numerous lakes.

Dominating the landscape in various stages of geologic splendor are the snowcapped peaks to the west. In order from north to south, they are Mount Jefferson, Mount Washington, North Sister, Middle Sister, South Sister, and last but not least even with its forlorn name, Broken Top.

Hiking is one of the best ways to fully appreciate the diversity of this region of Oregon. There are actually four distinct geographic zones all observable at once: 1) the high alpine slopes of the volcanoes, with meadows of wildflowers and crumbling lava rock; 2) subalpine forests of ponderosa pine and mountain hemlock nourished by cascading streams and glacial lakes; 3) steep-walled canyons that protect the last of the old-growth fir; and 4) arid pockets of lodgepole pine interspersed with bear grass.

Besides foot travel, other ways to take in the scenery are by horseback or mountain bike. Retrace the routes of such early-day explorers as Lewis and Clark, Kit Carson, and John Fremont on the Metolius-Windigo Trail. Outfitters in Sisters can help you with any hoofed mode of travel.

For cyclists, a 30-mile loop trip along the crest of Green Ridge provides panoramic views of the Cascades. It's a climb of 1,700 feet to the top, and it would be advisable to have a map of the route as you ride. This is good advice for anyone who plans to explore places not in the immediate vicinity of Forest Service Road 14 along the Metolius. There is a crazy network of spur roads that can easily lead you astray if you don't know your way around.

Highlights of a stay at Riverside Campground include short walks to Metolius Spring and Jack Creek Spring, the Metolius River Canyon near Camp Sherman, and the Wizard Falls Fish Hatchery.

To get there, take SR 126/U.S. 20 (Santiam Highway) north of Sisters to its intersection with FS 14 (Camp Sherman Road). Turn right, and follow FS 14 around the base of Black Butte to FS 900. The camp is less than a mile north on this road. There are some services in Camp Sherman.

KEY INFORMATION

Riverside Campground
c/o Sisters Ranger District
P.O. Box 248
Sisters, OR 97759

Operated by: Deschutes National Forest

Information: (541) 549-2111

Open: Mid-April to mid-October

Individual sites: 16

Each site has: Picnic table, fire grill

Some sites have: Shade trees

Site assignment: First come, first served; no reservations

Registration: Self-registration on site

Facilities: Vault toilets, piped water

Parking: At access road, roughly 200 to 400 yards from campground; short walk-in to campsites

Fee: No fee

Elevation: 3,000 feet

Restrictions:

Pets–On leash

Fires–In fire pits only

Alcoholic beverages–Permitted

Vehicles–RVs up to 21 feet; no hookups

Other–14-day limit on stay

EAST

TWO PAN CAMPGROUND

Lostine, Oregon

Tucked away in the far northeastern corner of Oregon on a broad, grassy plain that once was the beloved homeland of the proud Nez Perce Indians sits a magical little kingdom of imposing granite peaks, flower-choked meadows, rushing glacial creeks, and crystalline alpine air.

Eagle Cap Wilderness, rising high above the Wallowa Valley in the Wallowa Mountains, is regularly referred to as "America's Little Switzerland" and even sports a Matterhorn of its own. Various sources list the peak's elevation anywhere between 9,832 feet and 10,004 feet (about 5,000 feet shorter than its European counterpart). Depending on whose measurement you trust, this makes the Matterhorn the highest point in Eagle Cap.

Following close on its heels, however, are several dozen other peaks above 8,000 feet. In fact, Oregon has 29 peaks that are 9,000 feet or higher. Seventeen of them are clustered in Eagle Cap, the largest wilderness tract in Oregon at more than 350,000 acres.

The road to Two Pan follows the Lostine River south, piercing deep into the Wallowa range and gaining altitude steadily once it enters the canyon. The drive up from the valley floor and into the canyon is an education in both the geology and history of the area. About a million years ago, a large glacier carved out the

CAMPGROUND RATINGS

Beauty:	★★★★★
Site privacy:	★★★
Site spaciousness:	★★★★
Quiet:	★★★★★
Security:	★★★★
Cleanliness/upkeep:	★★★★★
Insect control:	★★ (summer)
	★★★★ (off-season)

Of the choices for getting to the Wallowa Mountains—"America's Little Switzerland"—and the magnificent terrain supporting them, Two Pan Campground affords one of the best jumping-off spots for extended backpacking.

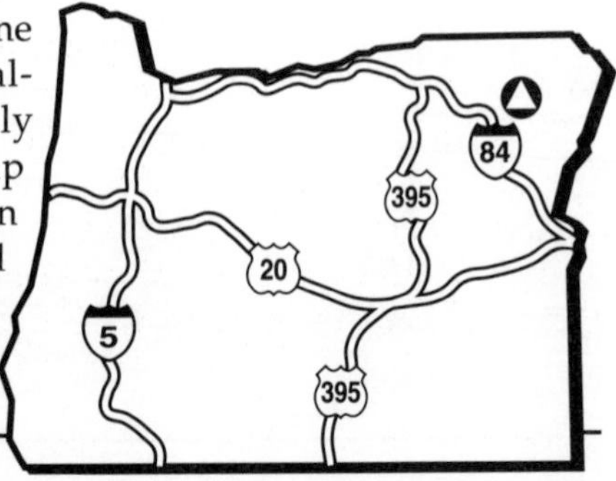

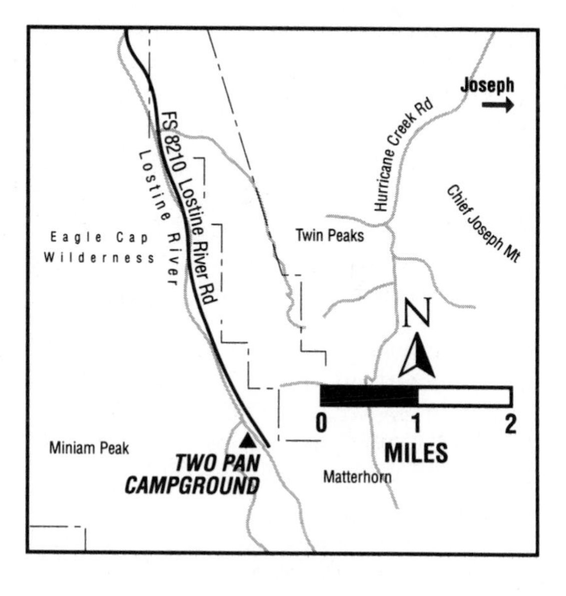

Lostine River Canyon as it advanced down from the center of the Wallowa Mountains. Grass-covered mounds in the lowlands, known as moraines, are the rock and soil deposits left by the glacier in its advance-and-melt periods over hundreds of years. Geologists estimate by measuring the height of the moraines that ice as thick as 400 feet once covered this area.

Pole Bridge Picnic Area (a bit past the national forest boundary) is the site of an old bridge, constructed entirely of poles, that once crossed the river here. About all that's left is a piece of foundation, but it makes a good reason to stop. Fortify yourself for the remainder of the drive with a snack and observe more glacial activity in the deep gorge that the river has cut into the canyon. This is about half a mile up from the picnic grounds.

Two miles farther is an even better opportunity to view the natural beauty of the Wild and Scenic Lostine River. A short trail takes you to an overlook of Lostine Gorge, a dramatic plunge between steep canyon walls where vegetation works hard to survive despite the predominant tumble of rocks and boulders.

The Wallowa Mountains were once the site of busy gold and silver mining. The ramshackle remains of cabins and outbuildings on the privately held Lapover Ranch (Mile 16) are all that is left of mining claims established by Kansas settlers in 1911. They got in just under the wire—the Wallowa National Forest received its federal designation later that same year.

You'll be tempted to drink straight from the cold, gushing river to quench your thirst. Keep in mind, however, that mountain goats, bighorn sheep, elk, deer, and a variety of smaller wild animals inhabit all areas of Eagle Cap. The risk of diarrhea from giardiasis is ever-present. Better to boil or treat the glacial flow, unfortunate as that may seem.

If you want seclusion on your exploration of Eagle Cap Wilderness, avoid the Lakes Basin region, which gets overrun by the crowds from Wallowa Lake. If you want to avoid the mosquitoes and biting flies (which are as thick in midsummer as the crowds), go in September. If you want to treat yourself after roughing it in the wilds, stop in at Wallowa Lake Lodge (on the south shore at the end of State Route 82). This fine old resort offers pleasant rooms, fine dining, and lively banter with the friendly staff.

To get there from Lostine (10 miles west of Enterprise on SR 82), follow Lostine River Road due south all the way to its end at the campground (18 miles). Lostine River Road becomes FS 8210 at the national forest boundary, about halfway to the campground.

KEY INFORMATION

Two Pan Campground
c/o Eagle Cap Ranger District
P.O. Box 907
Baker, OR 97814

Operated by: Wallowa-Whitman National Forest

Information: (541) 523-1205 or the ranger district at (541) 426-4978

Open: Mid-June to November

Individual sites: 6

Each site has: Picnic table, fire grill

Site assignment: First come, first served; no reservations

Registration: Not necessary

Facilities: Vault toilets, covered corral with hitch rack, no piped water

Parking: In campground

Fee: No fee

Elevation: 5,600 feet

Restrictions:

Pets–On leash

Fires–In fire pits only

Alcoholic beverages–Permitted

Vehicles–No RV or trailer accommodations

APPENDICES

APPENDIX A
Camping Equipment Checklist

Except for the large and bulky items on this list, I keep a plastic storage container full of the essentials of car camping so that they're ready to go when I am. I make a last-minute check of the inventory, resupply anything that's low or missing, and away I go!

Cooking Utensils
Bottle opener
Bottles of salt, pepper, spices, sugar, cooking oil, and maple syrup in waterproof, spill-proof containers
Can opener
Corkscrew
Cups, plastic or tin
Dish soap (biodegradable), sponge, and towel
Flatware
Food of your choice
Frying pan
Fuel for stove
Matches in waterproof container
Plates
Pocketknife
Pot with lid
Spatula
Stove
Tin foil
Wooden spoon

First Aid Kit
Band-Aids
First aid cream
Gauze pads
Ibuprofen or aspirin
Insect repellent
Moleskin
Snakebite kit (if you're heading for desert conditions)
Sunscreen/chapstick
Tape, waterproof adhesive

Sleeping Gear
Pillow
Sleeping bag
Sleeping pad, inflatable or insulated
Tent with ground tarp and rainfly

Miscellaneous
Bath soap (biodegradable), washcloth, and towel
Camp chair
Candles
Cooler
Deck of cards
Fire starter
Flashlight with fresh batteries
Foul weather clothing (useful year-round in the Northwest)
Paper towels
Plastic zip-top bags
Sunglasses
Toilet paper
Water bottle
Wool blanket

Optional
Barbecue grill
Binoculars
Books on bird, plant, and wildlife identification
Fishing rod and tackle
Hatchet
Lantern
Maps (road, topographic, trails, etc.)

APPENDIX B
Information

The following is a partial list of agencies, associations, and organizations to write or call for information on outdoor recreation opportunities in Oregon and Washington.

OREGON

AAA Automobile Club of Oregon
600 SW Market
Portland, OR 97201
(503) 222-6700

Bureau of Land Management
P.O. Box 2965, Portland, OR 97232
1300 NE 44th, Portland, OR 97213
(503) 280-7001

Crater Lake National Park (National Park Service)
P.O. Box 7
Crater Lake, OR 97604
(503) 594-2211

Hells Canyon National Recreation Area (U.S. Forest Service)
P.O. Box 490
Enterprise, OR 97828
(503) 426-3151

The Mazamas (hiking and climbing club)
909 NW 19th Street
Portland, OR 97209
(503) 227-2345

Nature of Oregon Information Center (maps and field guides)
800 NE Oregon, #5
Portland, OR 97232
(503) 731-4444

Oregon Coast Association
P.O. Box 670
Newport, OR 97365
(503) 336-5107
(800) 982-6278 (toll free in Oregon)

Oregon Department of Fish and Wildlife
506 SW Mill Street
Portland, OR 97208
(503) 229-5403

Oregon Economic Development Department, Tourism Division
775 Summer Street, NE
Salem, OR 97310
(503) 378-3451
(800) 547-7842 (toll free nationwide)

Oregon State Parks and Recreation Division
525 Trade Street, SE
Salem, OR 97310
(503) 378-8605

Campsite Information Center
3554 SE 82nd
Portland, OR 97266
(503) 731-3411 (within Portland city limits and outside Oregon)
(800) 452-5687 (toll free outside Portland city limits within Oregon; March through August)

Outdoor Recreation Information Center (National Park Service and U.S. Forest Service information for Washington, Oregon, and Idaho)
915 Second Avenue, Room 442
Seattle, WA 98174
(206) 220-7450

U.S. Fish and Wildlife Service (Oregon office)
P.O. Box 111
Lakeview, OR 97630
(503) 947-3315

U.S. Forest Service (Pacific Northwest Regional Headquarters)
P.O. Box 3623, Portland, OR 97208
319 SW Pine, Portland, OR 97208
(503) 221-2877

WASHINGTON

AAA Automobile Club of Washington
330 Sixth Avenue, North
Seattle, WA 98109
(206) 448-5353

Cascade Bicycle Club
444 NE Ravenna Blvd.
Seattle, WA 98105
(206) 522-3222
(206) 522-BIKE (ride description hotline)

Coulee Dam National Recreation Area (National Park Service)
P.O. Box 7
Coulee Dam, WA 99116
(509) 633-9441

Mount Rainier National Park (National Park Service)
Tahoma Woods, Star Route
Ashford, WA 98304
(206) 569-2211

Mount St. Helens National Volcanic Monument (U.S. Forest Service)
42218 NE Yale Bridge Road
Amboy, WA 98601
(206) 247-5473
(206) 274-4038 (visitor center; 24-hour information)

The Mountaineers (hiking and climbing club)
300 Third Avenue, West
Seattle, WA 98119
(206) 284-6310

North Cascades National Park (National Park Service)
2105 Highway 20
Sedro Woolley, WA 98284
(206) 856-5700

Northwest Interpretive Association (nonprofit information service)
83 South King Street, Suite 212
Seattle, WA 98104
(206) 553-7958

Olympic National Park (National Park Service)
600 East Park Avenue
Port Angeles, WA 98362
(206) 452-4501

Outdoor Recreation Information (National Park Service and U.S. Forest Service information for Washington, Oregon, and Idaho)
915 Second Avenue, Room 442
Seattle, WA 98174
(206) 220-7450

Washington Kayak Club
P.O. Box 24264
Seattle, WA 98124
(206) 433-1983

Washington State Department of Commerce and Economic Development, Tourism Division
P.O. Box 42513
Olympia, WA 98504
(800) 544-1800 (toll free nationwide)

Washington State Department of Fisheries
P.O. Box 43141
Olympia, WA 98504-3141
(206) 586-1425
(206) 976-3200 (Fisheries hotline)

Washington State Department of Natural Resources
P.O. Box 47031
Olympia, WA 98504-7031
(206) 902-1234

Washington State Department of Wildlife
600 Capitol Way, North
Olympia, WA 98501
(206) 753-5700

Washington State Parks and Recreation Commission
P.O. Box 42650
Olympia, WA 98504-2650
(206) 753-2027

Washington Trails Association
1305 Fourth Avenue
Seattle, WA 98101
(206) 625-1367

APPENDIX C
Suggested Reading and Reference

Barney's Book on the Olympic Peninsula. Arender, Barney. Nosado Press, 1990.

Bicycling the Backroads series. Woods, Erin and Bill. The Mountaineers. Most current editions.

Bicycling the Oregon Coast. Cody, Robin. Umbrella Books, 1990.

Exploring Oregon's Wild Areas. Sullivan, William. The Mountaineers, 1988.

Exploring Washington's Past. Alexander, Carmela and Kirk, Ruth. University of Washington Press, 1990.

Fishing in Oregon, Seventh Edition, Revised and Updated. Casali, Dan and Diness, Madelynne. Flying Pencil Publications, 1988.

Footsore 1, 2, 3, and 4. Manning, Harvey and Penny. The Mountaineers. Most current editions.

The Good Rain. Egan, Timothy. Alfred A. Knopf, Inc., 1990.

The Great Northwest Nature Factbook. Saling, Ann. Alaska Northwest Books, 1991.

Hiking the North Cascades. Darvill, Fred T. The Sierra Club, 1982.

Listening for Coyote. Sullivan, William. Henry Holt and Company, 1988.

Mountain Bike Adventure series. Kirkendall, Tom. The Mountaineers, 1989.

One Hundred Hikes series. Manning, Harvey and Spring, Ira. The Mountaineers. Most current editions.

Oregon Geographic Names. McArthur, Lewis L. Western Imprints: The Press of the Oregon Historical Society, 1982.

Oregon's Quiet Waters. McLean, Cheryl and Brown, Clint. Jackson Creek Press, 1987.

The Pacific Crest Trail, Volume 2: Washington and Oregon, Fifth Edition. Schaffer, Jeffrey P. and Selters, Andy. Wilderness Press, 1990.

Pacific Northwest Camping, Second Edition. Stienstra, Tom. Foghorn Press, 1990.

Quick Escapes in the Pacific Northwest. McFarlane, Marilyn. Globe Pequot Press, 1991.

Roadside Geology of Oregon, Second Edition. Alt, David D. Mountain Press Publishing Company, 1981.

Roadside Geology of Washington. Alt, David and Hyndman, Donald. Mountain Press Publishing Company, 1984.

Soggy Sneakers: Guide to Oregon Rivers, Second Edition. Willamette Kayak & Canoe Club, 1986.

Walks of the Pacific Northwest. Ferguson, Gary. Prentice Hall Press, 1991.

Washington Whitewater: The 34 Best Whitewater Rivers. North, Douglas. The Mountaineers, 1992.

A Waterfall Lover's Guide to the Pacific Northwest. Plumb, Gregory. The Mountaineers, 1989.